D0433946

ANQUETIL, *Alone*

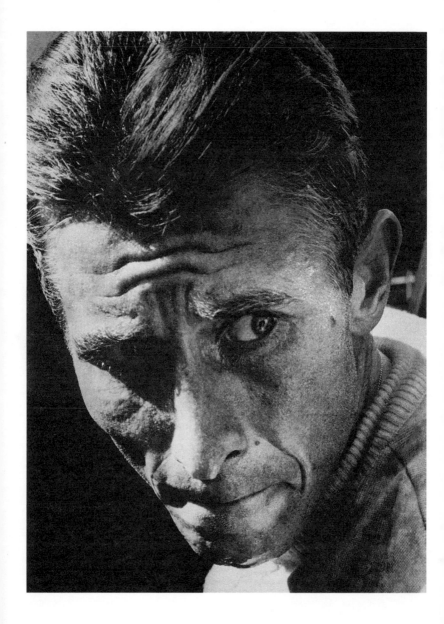

ANQUETIL, *Alone*

PAUL FOURNEL

Translated from the French
by Nick Caistor

 PURSUIT

First published in Great Britain in 2017 by
PURSUIT
An imprint of Profile Books Ltd
3 Holford Yard
Bevin Way
London
WC1X 9HD
www.profilebooks.com

First published in French in 2012 by
Editions du Seuil, entitled *Anquetil tout seul*

Translation copyright © Profile Books, 2017
Copyright © Editions du Seuil, 2012
Frontispiece photograph © DR

1 3 5 7 9 10 8 6 4 2

Typeset in Granjon by MacGuru Ltd
Printed and bound in Great Britain by Clays, St Ives plc

A CIP catalogue record for this book is available from the British Library.

ISBN 978 1 78125 731 9
eISBN 978 1 78283 298 0

Geldermans told me that before every climb, Anquetil used to take his water bottle out of its holder and stick it in the back pocket of his jersey to lighten his bike. I decided to look more closely. I discovered that, in all the photos of Anquetil in the mountains, the bottle was in its holder. But that was an illusion: Geldermans' story is the true one. That's the one that gets to the heart of the cyclist. It's the photos that are lying.

Tim Krabbé, *The Rider*

Over-exertion is a vain notion for cyclists.

Antoine Blondin

A reactor, an IBM machine and a spirit-still.

Raphaël Geminiani, *Les années Anquetil*

Anquetil enjoyed the blessing of the winds. His pointed nose and face like a fine blade sliced the road open for him, and his whole body flowed behind it, cutting through the mistrals, piercing the winter breezes and the summer storms. He seemed to be diaphanous, almost ill, with a slender build that was half a Van Looy, a third of Rudi Altig. His profile was like one on a medal, and when you saw him looking so slight you would never have imagined he had such a barrel chest, a barrel hiding the gunpowder of the most explosive engine, or that his legs and lower back were made of latex.

The way he pedalled was a lie. It spoke of ease and grace, like a bird taking off or a dancer in a sport of lumberjacks, riders who crushed the pedals, gluttons for hard work, masculinity in all shapes and sizes. Anquetil pedalled blond, with supple ankles; he pedalled on points, back bent, arms at right angles, head straining forwards. No man was ever better suited than him to riding a bike, never was the harnessing of man and machine so harmonious. He was made to be seen alone on the road, silhouetted against the blue sky; nothing about him suggested the peloton, the crowd and the strength of being united. He was cycling beauty, out on its own. 'For a long while I thought of him as a sorcerer who has found the Great Secret', Cyrille Guimard said of him. From his first turn of the pedal, he exchanged the legendary toughness of the 'galley slaves of the road' for an unprecedented kind of violence, something that looked elegant but was secretly brutal, and from which his opponents were going to suffer, without being able to imitate him. It should be added that Anquetil doesn't grimace, bare his teeth, jerk his head as he struggles. He is hard to read. He simply turns pale, his face is imperceptibly sunken, his eyes turn light grey. At the hardest moments of a race, when he's going at 50 kph, you would think he was consumptive.

❧

I was ten years old. I was small, brown-haired and tubby. He was big, blond and slender, and I wanted to be him. I wanted his bike, his allure, his nonchalance, his elegance. I had found my model and my opposite wrapped into one. Both of these were impossible to achieve, which meant I had a long way to go.

❧

For Anquetil, the essential takes place in solitude. He doesn't like mass races, he doesn't like to show off. His opponents are there to be beaten; they aren't there to get

2

to know or to play games with. His team-mates are there to work hard to make him win and to earn their own livelihoods. Nothing more. There are things he does alone and things that he alone does. In both cases, solitude is his kingdom. This solitude is not simply a way of considering what cycling is about, it's an overall way of life, the defining characteristic of his soul, whether that has been sold to God or the Devil.

Against Himself

Anquetil is standing naked, balanced nervously over the bathtub as it fills with boiling water. The steam grips his sex, buttocks, legs: the precious calves, the golden thighs. The head receives the vapours, becomes a thermometer. Anquetil peers down at his feet, but can't see them. He absorbs the heat, gorges his muscles on it. He doesn't think of the race he's taking part in, doesn't go through the bends and contours in his mind. The outline is rolled up in his belly: he can feel it there, hard, compact, painful, knotty, and knows that soon, right after the start, it will unroll and follow every last centimetre, like the most detailed route map. He is scared. The steam swells his quadriceps and eases his torment. He has followed all the rituals one by one: he has had a haircut, well-groomed on top and trimmed well above the ears, like a grooved artillery shell ... he has been to see his healer, who laid his hands on his weak throat and all the parts of his body where he is going to feel pain beyond pain. On Friday, he rode the 120 kilometres of the ritual at the speed of his old trainer Boucher's motorbike, nestled in its shelter at the limits of his strength; on Saturday he dug the length of the course metre by metre, studying it on the map, taking in every detail; and now he is warming himself over the bathtub.

On the chair next to the washstand, the black shorts, white socks, his jersey – all of them brand new; the shoes with black leather soles, polished and already worn to avoid any nasty surprises, the cleats carefully nailed underneath. He won't be wearing a cap.

ANQUETIL: I'm wedded to the crown of the road, at its highest point, I don't cut across at the bends, saving myself having to descend and climb back all the time. I leave that line to the cheapskates, the penny-pinchers. I retrace the road-builder's design and his pure line, choose the part that vehicles have worn smooth, leaving the edges to flints, shards of glass, dust. The road glides beneath my stomach. I've learned all about it on the rim of my wheels. I know that after this house it will turn left and start to climb, I know this stand of trees below will protect me from the wind for a moment. The whole width of the road is mine, and I trace the cleanest path along it that I can. The narrowest tubulars have been inflated to 10 bars, and I'm flying on my path of air.

I love fine-grained roads, broad, well-designed ones where you can give it all you've got, the wide, flat bends, gentle ups and downs … the climbs where you can start and then build your effort without losing speed. Picardy, Châteaufort, the long level stretches across the wheat fields of Chevreuse combed by the wind. Lower your chest still further, barely raise the eyes to spot the horizon rather than actually look at it, split open the air with the bridge of the nose. 52 × 15, 52 × 14, 52 × 13. The road glides beneath my stomach like an endless black ribbon. I live on the road. My houses, my châteaux are stopovers.

The wind is solid matter I plunge into, rounded back, nose pointed at the centre of the handlebars, arms stuck to my sides. An immobile egg fitted with connecting rods. Even at the most difficult moments, when my body is so taut it becomes unbearable, I force myself not to change my posture an inch. My back is crying out but I pull even harder on the pedals. Simply to raise my head for an instant to relieve the pain in the nape of my neck would cost me seconds. In any position, nothing is dearer than disorder. Skiers have taught me that.

I never tire of telling journalists my secret: in a time trial you have to start flat out, finish flat out, and in between take a moment to catch your breath, snatch some rest, a few kilometres where the pressure is lowered and strength is rebuilt before the final sprint. Of course, I never do that, but I tell anyone willing to listen that's what I do. My rivals all end up trying the same. 'Maybe he's right. Maybe that's the secret of his strength.' They lift off the pedal for an instant, and that always gives me the edge. While they're slowing down, I go flat out from start to finish. I am a machine, an escaped robot. I attack. I have fork-arms, connecting-rod thighs. I'm free.

I'm hurting. The nape of the neck, shoulders, kidneys, and then there's the hell of buttocks and thighs. You have to resist the burning sensation, the knotted muscles, the stabbing pain that returns with every turn of the pedal, be alert to the instant where there's a risk of paralysing cramp setting in. Resist the lead that is added to your muscles every quarter of an hour of the race. Keep your mind clear to make sure the movement is always complete: push, pull, lift, slam down, never forget to make the roundest circle. To pedal properly, raise the ankle. Switch to the biggest gear possible as quickly as possible, and stick with it. Don't listen to the body and head uniting to tell you this has to stop right now. Pedal in a world of pain of which only I know the secret, and convince myself that if I am suffering so much it's impossible for the others to keep up.

I've stocked up on pain. In training, behind Boucher's derny, behind Janine's Mercedes, or even in front of it when she is pushing me on. At 60 kilometres per hour, I'm going faster than in a race, faster than myself. I train in pain. My trainers aren't allowed to slow down, they have to pull me into zones of suffering that I alone know of. Even if I beg them to, they are not to slacken the pace. Clench your teeth, keep going, never put your hands behind your back. On race day, when I'm on my own and am suffering like a dog, I know that deep inside I'm aware of much worse pain. This gives me the slight edge that allows me to hurt myself more than the other cyclists. The harder the race, the more I can feel the others' pain, and that soothes mine.

Behind me, on the bumper of the maroon Hotchkiss or the white 203 Peugeot, my name is painted in capitals so that the public will recognise me. Black letters on a white background: ANQUETIL. My name pursues me and pushes me on. I am on my own heels. Fleeing myself.

In the distance, at the end of the straight line, the lead vehicle swerved to one side, and I saw Poulidor, who had set off three minutes ahead of me. I caught a glimpse of his purple jersey, the Mercier team colours. My eyes impaled his back like a harpoon; now I've got him. He's going to pull me in on the line that has just been stretched between us. He set off three minutes before me and yet there he is, already within reach. The road bends now and hides him from me, his support car conceals him, but I'm not letting him go. He's going to reel me in. Now is the right moment. In the next few minutes I'm not going to ask myself any more questions. I'm being sucked along. I've already gained a good kilometre per hour just at the thought of catching him. It'll soon be two kilometre per hour. At the next straight, my eyes will be fixed on his purple shoulders and he'll pull me in even more. To take full advantage of his strength, I need to accelerate steadily. I have to resist the desire to go flat out; I want to leave him in my wake. I leave one side of the road to him; I'm going to overtake on his left, sweep past without looking at him, my eyes on the tarmac, making sure not to move a millimetre in the saddle. My speed will crush all his hopes. He's bound to turn his head to the left, give me a worried look. He's done for. 'I've already lost three minutes', he'll tell himself. My legs have to be the only moving part of my body. He doesn't count. All Poulidor will feel is the rush of wind.

My wind. I won't turn my head. I mustn't meet his gaze. He doesn't exist. Only the road exists and I'm back in the crown of the road. I pass him. Completely.

He's behind me. He reeled me in, now he has to push me on. I still need to use his strength. Pretend I am scared: imagine he's fighting back, that he's going to catch me, remember Albert Bouvet who resisted me for a while on the Côte de Bullion, pedal harder still until I feel the line snap at last and imagine Poulidor swallowed up in the depths of the road all alone, emptied of himself. And now think of nothing but the rider who left six minutes before me, the one my eyes are already searching for at the far end of the straight line.

This scene takes place during a time trial between Bourgoin and Lyons (62 kilometres). Raymond Poulidor, who set off three minutes before Anquetil, is about to be caught. His trainer Antonin Magne ignores the regulations and pulls alongside him. Instead of shouting at him, he simply says: 'Move over Raymond, and watch the Caravel as it sails by.' And the two men watch the Caravel go by. 'I couldn't see him pedalling,' Poulidor confirms, 'he was gliding along.'

The Caravel glided through my cycling childhood with a mysterious majesty. Too young to understand, I was old enough to admire. I feasted my eyes on this champion who was like a star in spiked shoes. I rode round and round my house, pedalling like a madman with my chubby legs and splayed feet, dreaming of the Grand Prix des Nations. I too contorted myself into the perfect position, back and neck bent at the ideal angle, bright red, jaw locked. I spent whole summers like that.

My cyclist father and bicycle-maker uncle had fashioned an ideal bike that perfectly met the twin demands of dreams and apprenticeship. It had all the appearance of a racing bike, combined with the prudence of a teaching machine (for a first-year pupil). Above all, and this was something I insisted on, it was green. I can still remember my glee when I first saw it at the far end of the dark workshop, glinting like a new penny piece, gleaming in the sparks of the soldering. Green, like Anquetil's. This was after several long, impatient weeks because in those days, around Saint-Étienne, you had to learn to wait for a bike to be custom-made. As the days went by, I had been to see first the frame itself, freshly forged, and then all the extras being added. I was on tenterhooks while it was enamelled and assembled. I waited and waited … until finally there it was, my own bike. I'd show them. I started racing against the clock, beating my own records on the paths around our house in the Haute-Loire. I did the whole loop in 'one or two minutes'. It's true that my watch had no second hand and I often wasted precious seconds when I dismounted to see what my time was when I was halfway round … but I had so much energy that these imprecise timings never threatened my utter domination of the Grand Prix des Nations. Soon I set off on the roads and my dreams expanded to fill the much vaster universe of the paths and roads beyond.

~

And we saw Anquetil. My father was a responsible admirer who willingly chose to cross France to see the great Jacques. The only condition was that he had to get there on his bike to better understand and share with him, in however small measure, the effort of cycling. I came across Anquetil on four occasions 'for real', in my childhood and adolescence, but he peopled all my day-dreams … my admiration was the clear-sighted admiration of a child cyclist. I preferred him to Poulidor, and that allowed me to analyse them both. In doing so I was behaving like most French people of that time, who chose one camp or the other – and above all Poulidor's.

Later, when other champions came along, when other ways of winning emerged, I began to ask myself questions. How had a champion like Anquetil been possible? How could someone like him have been such a devastating racer? Where once he had seemed so clear to me, he now became unfathomable, because he had been so different to the new champions I was discovering. Anquetil became an enigma, which I've been trying for a long, long time to decode, in search more of questions than answers, convinced that this inimitable model holds the secret of all the characteristics and contradictions that set a champion apart from everyone else.

Some champions appear as simple machines: they love their sport, then they love victory, and then the money that comes with it, glory, fame, comfort, all of which are magnificently and clearly understandable. Others, though, appear to be complex mechanisms, driven by contradictory forces, negative energies they have to overcome, to channel if not master, if they are to be turned into winners' bouquets. They accuse themselves of lack of willpower, cannot accept the evidence of their strength – and paradoxically this pushes them still further beyond the heights they had set themselves as goals. Among these champions, Anquetil is without doubt the most complete and the most complex. The one who in a group sport always succeeded in remaining the great model of the individual.

The organisers of the Grand Prix of Lugano, a superb time trial in the south of Switzerland, were pleased that Anquetil honoured them with his presence. If we are to believe the secrets that are the stuff of legend, they were not so delighted that he also honoured them with his power. He had already won six times and there was nothing to suggest he wouldn't win again this time. They therefore decided to ask him not to turn up. The reputation of their race could suffer. The Italian public needed some variety and, if possible, a winner who was one of them. Anquetil understood their problem only too well and, since they were paying his whole appearance fee for him not to start, he accepted with good grace.

A few months later, according to the rumour, the organisers thought better of it: Anquetil was multiplying his triumphs, and it seemed hard not to let him defend his title in front of their precious public. Taking a second payment, Anquetil agreed to go back on the decision he had been forced to make. He promised to be there. At the other end of the line, the organiser thanked him and took a deep breath. Now came the delicate moment.

'We're delighted to have you take part, dear Jacques, very honoured, but you know how the Italian *tifosi* are: they're hot-blooded and are dreaming of seeing one of their compatriots win … Perhaps you could …?'

'You want me to throw a time trial?'

'"To throw" is going a bit far, but perhaps you could refrain from exhibiting all your immense talent …'

'To lose.'

'Being beaten by someone as strong as you isn't exactly to lose.'

'As strong as me … How much?'

'Of course, we will be happy to pay you an extra fee.'

'Then it's possible. All I ask is for you to pay me up front, because at the finish I want to get away and not have to talk to journalists. I've got my reputation to consider.'

At the start of the Grand Prix the weather is lovely. The sight of the lake in the sunshine is magnificent, and Anquetil knows that, for once, he'll almost be able to enjoy it. He gets ready, pulling on his spotless white socks over his tanned calves. A few steps away from him, his wife Jacqueline is talking to Ercole Baldini. She likes Baldini, who is a worthy champion and a charming man. Only Anquetil can beat him in a race like this, which means that today he is going to be the winner of the Grand Prix of Lugano. Anquetil respects Baldini because like him he is a specialist in solo efforts, and is without a doubt the best Italian time-trial rider. He's in a playful frame of mind, with the weight of the course and the need to win lifted off his shoulders, although slightly heavy from a hearty meal. He goes over to Baldini.

'Tell me, Ercole, can you hold your tongue and say nothing to the organisers?'

'What a question.'

'If you give me your fee, I'll let you win.'

'You've had enough of it? And it makes you laugh! Of course I'll do it, and thanks very much.'

This means Anquetil collected his fourth appearance fee for a race he had promised to lose. As the weather was fine, the route beautiful and the prize money substantial, he won anyway. And Baldini understood that perfectly, because he knew how champions function – he was one himself, obviously not on top form that day, but still smiling. Racing is also a game, and you have to be really good to pull off such a stunt.

ANQUETIL: I'm hungry. To be good on a bike you have to be good at table and to enjoy life. I'm going to eat oysters and veal stew with a bottle of Gros Plant. It's sunny, the

Tour du Var is coming to an end, the stage is fine. It's eight o'clock in the morning, the astonished owner of the Hotel Mirabelle takes the order and complies without a fuss. He goes off to his stoves. He hasn't a second to lose, he knows I have to start the race in under two hours. My team-mates and rivals chew on a croissant, still half-asleep. Antonin Magne, Poulidor's manager, who is staying at the same hotel, hovers round me. I am his favourite mystery. He looks slightly ridiculous in the grey smock and Basque beret he always wears, like a cross between a country schoolteacher and an upmarket watch-maker. He is said to be full of cyclist lore. He knows the secrets of grilled steaks and boiled carrots, the secret of the team members sent ahead on breakaways in the mountain stages so that later on they can support their leader. He knows all there is to know about the sport, and he finds me extremely irritating. He can't bear my eight o'clock oysters; he detests my stew. He can't restrain himself, he has to teach me a lesson in public. There he goes, indignantly, in front of everyone, shouting and pointing at me: 'He may be Anquetil, but don't be surprised if he suffers from cramps!' I would have preferred him to come and sit down opposite me and tell it to me, and only me, right in my face. He exasperates me with his old schoolmaster's ways. I hate being disturbed when I'm eating, especially as the wine is chilled, and it's a pleasure to dip your bread in the thick sauce. Now I don't even have time for a dessert. I have to go and sign the stage card and then get to work between Sainte-Maxime and Saint-Tropez, in other words between holidays and holidays. I'm going to calm down, and as there's riding to do, I may as well do it pedalling. There'll be no slacking today, that's for sure. And since there are bound to be cramps, I'm going to start up the cramp-making machine. I'm going to create 120 kilometres of hell along the back roads, to the good health of Monsieur Magne. And at the finish I'm the one snatching the bouquet, simply to prove to them that cyclist lore is reinvented every morning. In its sauce.

～

September 1953. At the finish of his famous first Grand Prix des Nations, which brings him glory at the age of nineteen, Anquetil rushes to find Roger Creton. It's urgent. He has to make it up to him at once, to find the little rider from Rouen, who only the week before had been his rival. He has to find him because he's no longer a rival, because the world has been turned upside down in a single race. All of a sudden Anquetil has become immense, and friends from his part of the country have to remain friends because now the rivals will come from all over. Creton: where is Creton? That's the new star's first concern. He has just proved that he has the greatest talent imaginable: a champion is born fully equipped, skipping the years of learning and training, the preparatory races ... and here he is, looking for Creton, the obscure little Norman rider he had a stupid quarrel with. There he is: let's be friends. And Creton is only too pleased, he's no longer angry at all, he's delighted. Now he's the friend of a real champion, and waxes lyrical: 'From now on,' he

says, 'your name will shine in the firmament of cycling.'
That Creton knows what he's talking about.

⁓

One sunny morning, I'm training on the narrow road
just outside our house, in the countryside. Straddling
my green racer, Anquetil perfects his posture for a time
trial. His aim is to reduce my frontal area as much as
possible to achieve efficient air-streaming. He lowers his
head, pulls it into his shoulders and presses on my pedals. He accelerates. To be sure my skull isn't raised, he
stares down at his front wheel. The road slips by underneath. The sense of speed is so great he regrets not having any toe clips to help him pull on the pedals when he
lifts his legs, and so gain a few extra kilometres per hour.
He is wondering how to improve his breathing despite
his aching lungs and straining guts when suddenly he
is thrown to the ground. His race ends in a heap on the
gravel of the road, warm blood running down his face
and leg. He finds himself upended in his bike frame, his
pedals, and spilled baskets of vegetables. A large lady
in black is sitting next to him in the road, rubbing her
backside. Her bike is in the ditch, handlebars twisted,
her heavy load scattered all over the tarmac. 'What are
you doing riding on the left without looking, my boy?'
she asks sourly.

Anquetil escapes with a few stitches and some
lame excuses. But even today no one knows who let that
market-gardening woman loose on his training route.

Devious organisers? Antonin Magne? Still a complete mystery.

For every champion there has to be the story of the smooth-cheeked adolescent, sitting on an improbable bicycle, who has just outdone his much better equipped elders on the climbs, heralding future victories. In Anquetil's case, this wasn't quite how things happened: at the age of nineteen, even before he is a professional cyclist, he takes part in the famous Grand Prix des Nations, the longest and most prestigious annual time trial and, racing on his own for the whole 140 kilometres, he beats everyone else by more than six minutes. He smashes the record set by the great Hugo Koblet and passes, without any apprenticeship, at 39.630 kph, from being a child to being a star (and this will leave its mark). Anquetil takes a sledgehammer to the history of cycling.

Immediately, doubts arise. There's no denying the kid looks great on his bike, but he is too slender, almost transparent. He doesn't give the impression either of health or strength. 'Anquetil, an independent French cyclist, thin, pale but magnificently built, demonstrated a powerful, fluid action that was a pleasure to watch', writes an English journalist, sensitive to the young man's almost feminine charm. But the questions keep arising, the doubts surface: 'The kid has class, but is he healthy?' the dailies speculate.

The experts, though, disregard his pale features,

his apparent fragility, and instead look at the stats: 1.76 metres tall, 70 kilos in weight, lung capacity of six litres, 48 heartbeats a minute. All of which adds up to a very solid basis.

～

No sooner has he won a victory than Anquetil piles on the pressure: in October 1953, a few weeks after his first triumph as a professional, he decides to go and meet Coppi in person. The visit might seem like the banal flight of fancy of a very young fan who admires his favourite great champion, but in fact this anodyne excursion couldn't be more loaded with intention. Anquetil has not come on a visit, he's not there to declare his allegiance: he's there simply to set the bar at the proper height. *His* bar. He doesn't expect anything from Coppi, he has come to Novi Ligure to measure his own ambition and to put himself under a pressure that will last throughout his career. He is not bothered about being just another racing cyclist; what he wants is to be Coppi, the *campionissimo*, nothing less. That is what this unexpected trip tells us. Will he address him politely, or use the familiar form of verbs to speak to him as a friend and equal?

I would have given anything to be a good enough cyclist to go and see Anquetil in the same way in Normandy. I think I would have addressed him as a friend and equal. I knew him so well.

So Anquetil sets off in his brand-new Simca Châtelaine. He takes a bike with him to practise climbing in the mountains on his way there. On this journey, everything is thrown together and improvised, everything is done on impulse, and yet all the same Anquetil takes with him Vavasseur, the photographer for the *Ouest-France* newspaper. He wants this meeting to be recorded. He crosses the Alps, half pedalling, half driving, and then swoops down towards the plain of the River Po.

In his spacious mansion at Novi Ligure, Coppi receives him without ceremony. He is stretched out on the massage table, half-naked, his body pale down to the forearms and the middle of his thighs. He's just back from training. He is thin, almost slender, with legs that never seem to end. Apart from his thinness and his cylindrical chest, his body apparently holds no mystery. Anquetil is not particularly impressed.

He is more struck by the enormous giant in dark glasses leaning over Coppi. He is ferociously pummelling the *campionissimo* with his paddle-hands, kneading his muscles like a stony-faced baker. He doesn't say a word, or turn his head towards the newcomer.

Coppi greets Anquetil and thanks him for the visit. He knows all about his recent successes and takes him very seriously: for a professional like him the times the kid has set do not lie. Anquetil is struck by the champion's kindness. Doubtless he finds it hard to see in him the greatest cyclist of all time, the famous star whose public life is splashed across front pages all round the world, the man whose destiny is played out in black and white like a neo-realist Italian film: white for the White Lady who is his forbidden companion; white like his crazy solitary breakaways towards the snowy peaks of European mountains, black like the glasses worn by Cavanna, the blind masseur poring over him, black like his defeats in countless instances of 'one race too many', black like the medicine bag at the foot of the massage table.

He will be Coppi.

He is fascinated by Cavanna, the pummeller, the confidant, the guru, the supplier. A former heavyweight boxer, former track racer who has lost his sight but is, so they say, capable of recognising true champions just by feeling their muscles. He was the one who 'made' Coppi, it is whispered, when he was nothing more than a skinny adolescent.

Coppi has no doubts about the young visitor's class, but he gestures to Cavanna to make sure. Cavanna grabs hold of Anquetil and gives him a medical check-up. He palpates him roughly all over, gauging him and weighing him up with both hands, rolling his muscles in his fingers, digging for his vital organs beneath the skin. He finds a lot of Coppi in him: the same apparent fragility, the same strong back, same endless legs. No doubt he can also feel under the skin the willpower and determination, the moral toughness. He may be blind, but nothing escapes him. He concentrates for a long while on the youngster's pulse: he has a slow heartbeat. He places a hand gently on Anquetil's belly and concludes: 'You have a good stomach. Don't eat too much, do as Bobet does.'

What is Coppi's decision? Now he is sure that this young man is crammed with as many certainties as promise, now he is sure that his talent is not a mere flash in the pan, he can do no less than offer him work: to stay on top it's always good to have the strongest on your side. Coppi knows he is ageing and that he won't be able to match Anquetil, but he hopes to be the one who decides what share of the cake he'll have to offer him … he declares himself ready to advise him, help him, plan his training schedules, offer him both technical and financial means.

He gets dressed and takes Anquetil to visit his incubator for champions, a kind of hostel for cyclists he has set up with Cavanna in Novi Ligure. He lets it be understood that if Anquetil puts his trust in him, his future as a champion is assured.

Touched and polite, Anquetil hears him out but turns him down without hesitation. He knows the path he is going to take. It's out of the question for him to follow the Bobet diet, and to become the *campionissimo* himself he has above all to devour Coppi, starting by swallowing his unsurpassable world hour record. So he chooses to fight.

ANQUETIL: Riding in the peloton demoralises me. I don't know all these people around me; there's danger everywhere, I feel trapped. I hate my trainers who want me to lead from the front, I hate Darrigade. He's always the one who slips to the rear where I'm gently pedalling along and brings me back into line with news from the front of the race:

'Come on, wake up, you have to move up.'

'Leave me alone, I'm going over my accounts.'

'You can do them tonight. There's trouble up in front. Get on my wheel.'

And he pulls me up through the peloton. I slip in behind him and don't let him get a wheel away from me. To climb up through the peloton isn't easy: everybody wants to keep their place at the front so that they'll be in a good position when things speed up, and nobody sees any reason to let those from behind get past them. There's no way you can force your way through the middle: there are too many riders, danger and ill will are everywhere. Dédé takes me along the sides, where the mass of riders is more fluid, and you can even go on the inside, push your way through. There's no one like Dédé. The sprinters know how to 'rub', as they say in the peloton, and slip into mouse holes. And anyway, this is Monsieur Darrigade who's pulling Monsieur Anquetil. Which means that for some of the peloton at least it's worth making a bit of room.

The fact is, I don't like the riders in the pack. I can't even put a name to the faces of many of my colleagues. During the Tour I spotted one who was making break-aways the whole time and was getting on my nerves. I asked Dédé who he was, and he told me it was Adri-aenssens: 'A nasty customer. You have to keep your eye on him always. You must have been aware of him for a while now.' In fact, thinking about it, I only really like the peloton when it's a long way behind.

At moments of great solitude, I'm stronger than

all other men. This gift I nourish, the work I accumulate, these are my trademark, my glory, my fortune, my chateaux and my prison. When I'm not struggling alone against the clock and the wind, I pass the time inventing ways to escape.

I only have to feel that a wall is keeping me prisoner to want to jump over it. It's a reflex. If cigarettes are banned, I smoke. If we're not to go out at night, I go out. If flirting is outlawed, I flirt. Cycling is not my sport. I didn't choose it; the bike chose me. I don't love the bike, the bike loves me. It's going to pay for it.

On 29 June 1956, Anquetil enters the Vigorelli velodrome in Milan. It's empty, all his. This velodrome is reputed to be the fastest in Europe, the velodrome of records. Anquetil kneels down on the dark track and strokes it. Everything is soft. The light is good, the wood whispers of faraway places, Africa, Cameroon where it comes from, wide open spaces. The wind has dropped. It's here, on this track 397.39 metres long, that Anquetil is going to go round and round, caged in, for an hour, without moving his body, at the end of the end of suffering. An hour as fast as possible, at cycling's absolute limit. To Jacques, nothing is more beautiful than the hour record. There's no coming second: it's all or nothing. What's most difficult is not to race off too quickly right from the start, because an hour is endless. His task is a huge one: he has come to Italy to break Coppi's record. The oldest record in the world.

He has travelled in secret to train in the velodrome at Besançon. Not to test his strength, or to decide on a battle plan – he knows exactly what he can and must do – but to shatter his body, to send it a message about the profound, painful nature of what awaits him. This total effort has no equivalent in road racing. Anquetil knows he will not have a moment's respite, no relief on a descent or hill where he can relax, change position, or get his breath back. There is none of that on the track. The absolute of a single position maintained until it becomes torture, the absolute continuity of a rhythm each beat of which is controlled by a scoreboard that cannot be modified. An hour-long straight line, without moving the handlebars, with no countryside to look at, with only a sly tap on the head going into each banked corner.

On the first evening, at his first attempt, he suffers, and quits after fifty terrible minutes. Nothing is right: there are too many little sandbags marking the path at the edge of the track, and his bike is not responding as it should. He calls a halt before the hour is up. He knows he's not inside the record time. He analyses what went wrong and decides. He wants the same number of bags as there were for Coppi's record, placed in exactly the same way. And he wants exactly the same bike. Bianchi, the firm that supplies the *campionissimo*, is only too happy to offer him a fine bicycle. They are even ready to lend him Coppi's famous mechanic, Giuseppe De Grandi, known as Pinza d'Oro. But Anquetil is contracted to La Perle cycles and is only permitted to ride their machines. No matter: independent craftsmen in

Milan make him a bike with exactly the same specs as Coppi's in record time. A long frame, three-tenths steel, 110 gram silk tubulars, helium-filled, 28 spokes to each wheel, total weight 6 kilos. Anquetil will be able to fly.

On the second night, there are the right number of sandbags, and they are properly positioned. The bike, more elongated than his own, performs better on the banked bends. The velodrome is packed. The organiser would not hear of closing the gates. He put tickets on sale, but insisted on distributing flyers warning the public that they are coming at their own risk, and that a new world hour record cannot be guaranteed. This precaution is wasted, because one can imagine that the majority of the spectators have come to see Anquetil fail and to confirm their Coppi as the greatest of all time.

Anquetil is out on the track again. One hour of total concentration, absolute effort, and the world record, which has lasted for thirteen years, eight months and twenty-two days, explodes in front of the eyes of the astonished *tifosi*. Anquetil covers 46.159 kilometres in the hour, a whole lap more than Coppi. The lap of honour, as it were.

Anquetil doesn't crow. It's not in his nature, and he's not going to force it. He is happy of course, and yet maybe he feels a certain regret, a little pang. He didn't really want to beat the record so easily the first time. He would have preferred to beat it after several attempts, in order to raise the stakes each time. From now on, the record to beat is Anquetil's, and Anquetil himself will find it hard.

In the *gruppetto* of miniature plastic riders on my table, the yellow jersey was always Jacques Anquetil. Each evening I went over that day's stage. Different-sized books, spine upwards, like a coolie's hat, represented the third, second and first category climbs. Rulers and pencils marked the distances of the time trials. I was pleased to discover that one of my favourite sayings (by Anquetil), 'I like the long boring stretches of the flat stages', sounded like poetry. These endless flat stages were sheets of white paper. Battles exploded everywhere, and inevitably Bahamontes broke away on the climbs. At the summit, balancing on the back of the book, he enjoyed a strawberry ice cream while waiting for his colleagues to plunge into the descent. But Anquetil always came back at him. The script of the stage I had just seen on TV was written, and I could remember every single detail of it. I therefore followed it faithfully, and yet, if my memory serves me right, I think I tended to forget a few things towards the end of the race, forcing me to turn some results upside down, make a few substitutions, and a few other sleights of hand. Let's just say that the yellow jersey often had a definite tendency to win, thanks to a superhuman effort over the final kilometres. I have to admit that Anquetil's way of riding was already getting on my nerves.

In 1960, Anquetil was the first Frenchman to win the Giro d'Italia (I buy the little figure of him in the pink jersey). This was no mean feat if you think of the quality of the Italian opposition, especially Baldini and Nencini, and above all the passion of the muscular *tifosi*, unbeatable when it comes to transforming a climb into a lift service for their champions. Giving a push is at this period one of the fine arts of cycling, and the Italians are past masters at it: Bobet had bitter experience of this the previous year. As a safety measure, Anquetil therefore decides to get a good lead on the flat before they reach the mountains. He also wants to protect himself from the taciturn Luxembourger Charly Gaul, who is inspired by the mountain peaks and who, everyone agrees, perfectly fits his nickname as the Angel of the Mountains.

On 3 June, therefore, Anquetil decides to go on the attack in the time trial between Seregno and Lecco. This turns out to be one of the finest ever demonstrations of his strength. He demolishes the 68 kilometres at an average of more than 45 kph. He leaves Baldini at one minute 27 seconds behind him, and Gaul at more than six minutes. This is neither the first nor the last of his astonishing victories in time trials, but this one is timely because it comes the day before the climb up the terrifying Col de Gavia, and it's mysterious because it contains a secret. Anquetil always maintained that total concentration was the key to a successful solo effort – not to think of anything but the race, to focus on the effort, not to let your mind wander, or allow yourself to be invaded by your obsessions or your dreams … On this occasion, and as far as one can tell for the first and only time, he departs from this practice and allows himself to dream: 'As I rode along I told myself that if this had been a rest day rather than another stage, I would have gone to the Vigorelli track and tried to break the hour record. I saw myself in Milan, pushing hard on the pedals, not easing up a single instant.' To dream of riding while you're in a race, to dream of the hour record during a time trial, is a very strange sort of reverie for a so-called dilettante! I loved that story, and told it to my mates, who couldn't understand it at all. I trained to be able to dream of cycling as I rode. I've climbed so many mountains in that happy state.

During the race, the nights are often endless. The effect of the pills and stimulant injections won't wear off, the heart is still pounding and the night stretches on and on. After dinner, after chatting, after the game of cards where he has lost yet again, Anquetil goes for a walk in the street outside his hotel, alone in the darkness. The flotsam from the day's race is strewn all over the ground: the list of riders with their numbers, discarded advertising caps, cigarette butts, gifts, key rings, a big colour photograph of him that is hardly crumpled, only trodden on. He turns up the collar on his tracksuit. It's cold. It's the time of night when he wonders if he will still have the strength to start. He could stand in the middle of the road, holding his bike, and watch the peloton head off without him. He has the means, and at this time of night he almost wants to. He pauses on the finish line chalked on the tarmac: his life, his profession. This could be his last finish. He walks along it as if it were a high wire. He spreads his arms. On which side is he going to fall?

And yet when day dawns he'll go to eat and then sketch with the others an imaginary strategy for a race that will never exist. The ideal race, with no riders, no opponents, the race without a white line drawn across the tarmac. He'll put on a pair of new white socks, a clean blue jersey, black riding shorts. Will he start, or won't he?

ANQUETIL: Going up the Col du Luitel, I had no problem following Favero, but my legs hurt far more than usual. At Grenoble the rain came on even harder, and I realised I had made a mistake trying to be too clever. I should never have worn a silk jersey that morning. That's a jersey for the sun, for a victory, and now it's sticking to my skin like an icy straitjacket. Too late. You can't plan a deluge. The Col de Porte that starts just outside the town is dreadful. I feel dead. My lungs are filled with cotton wool. I'm gasping for breath like a fish tossed onto a grassy bank. I reach the big plateau, things should go better. But it gets worse. I try the low gear, but nothing happens. What's happened to my strength? What gear will I find it in? Geminiani overtakes me; I don't even have the courage to raise myself in the saddle to try to follow him. I stare at the road beneath me, but can't see it. Bobet draws alongside: 'Jacques, shall I wait for you?' 'No, Louis, it's not worth it.' I've always known to the second how I was doing, but now I can sense the minutes slipping away. I'm struggling: 5? 10? 15? 22? I'm scared on the descent, scared of myself. The cold has got into my hands. There are four others around me. I can't see them. I can feel their hands on my back. I cough, and spit. Spit red.

I am massaged, stretched out, the fever is too high for me to open my eyes. Doctor Dumas is sitting on the edge of my bed. He talks to me while I shiver. 'Jacques, I know you've had a light bike prepared for the time trial tomorrow, but I think you should abandon. You've got pneumonia. If you race, you'll end up in the clinic. Your health is at stake.' Through the fuzziness in my ears I hear 'pneumonia' and 'clinic'. I open my eyes for an instant: the bed is bathed in cold sweat. 'If I abandon, my team-mates will lose the team competition; the third rider is too far behind – they need me. They're going to lose three million.'

They do lose it. Anquetil coughs and spits blood.

⌒

Anquetil doesn't like lies. In 1961, he lines up again for the start of the Grand Prix des Nations. It is *his* race. He has already won it five times, and Paul Wiegant, his trainer at the time, wants him to achieve a new feat. Throughout the race, he gives him false time checks. He tells him he is twenty seconds behind schedule, then ten. Anquetil gets annoyed with the chronometer he always wears on his right wrist, and thinks it must be broken. He pushes even harder on the pedals, lost in his sensations.

He no longer knows where he is. He feels as though he is speeding along, but he's not gaining ground. If he is to believe Wiegant's checks, at 10 kilometres from the finish he is only equalling the previous year's time.

When he reaches the Parc des Princes, Anquetil discovers that in fact he has smashed his own record by one minute twenty seconds. He has left Desmet nine minutes behind, Moser at ten minutes, and Simpson at twenty! It's a colossal feat: Wiegant is over the moon. His ruse has worked; thanks to his subterfuge he has pushed his champion to the limits and beyond. At last he has converted his champion of economy into a king of debauch. The whole world now knows what Anquetil is capable of.

On the grass at the Parc des Princes, Anquetil says nothing. On the weighing machine that evening he discovers that he has lost five kilos over the 100 kilometres. He's exhausted, in a bad mood. Furious at having been fooled. He would have been more than happy with a few seconds' victory. His fury cools, but a truly Anquetil anger remains: a few weeks later, he decides to sack Wiegant and never to take part in the Grand Prix des Nations again.

⮯

The fourth and last time I truly saw Anquetil, I knelt down before him. I had just passed my first school certificate exams (in those days, we took two of them) and my parents, who were alongside me, had bought me a camera that I was about to christen. The weather was fine, the black-and-white film was brand new and properly inserted in the camera. It was 12 July 1964, and I was on the verge by the side of the road at two kilometres from the summit of the Puy de Dôme. The road was closed to cars, so we had climbed the mountain in the summer heat along with tens of thousands of other spectators. We were red from the sun and from our impatience. The rivalry between Anquetil and Poulidor was at its height, and the moment of truth was about to arrive. The fate of the Tour de France would be decided on this one climb. If Poulidor, who was said to be a better climber, managed to take a few seconds from Anquetil, he would finally don the yellow jersey, which he had never worn before. Otherwise, Anquetil would keep it. France back then was split in two, and as you can imagine, I was not among the Poulidor supporters who were shouting at the roadside. Thanks to a rumour that had spread up the ranks of spectators like a wave they had just heard that their champion, only a few cables' length below us, had at last managed to drop Maître Jacques.

First of all I photographed Poulidor. Then I waited a few seconds and knelt down so that I wouldn't miss Anquetil, who was climbing, chest heaving, face livid, at the extreme limit of his strength. Peering into my viewfinder, one knee pressed into the surface of the road, I was in a state of reverence. I was present at one of the greatest moments in the history of cycling, and I was photographing it!

Anquetil was tearing seconds from the tarmac, nose

to the crossbar, leaving his trail of sweat on the way up to the summit of the Puy de Dôme. By then I had more than enough experience as a cyclist to be able to say that he really wasn't going very fast. And that Poulidor, an instant before him, was not going very fast either.

If only I had been standing three hundred metres further down the mountain, I would have been the one to take the photo where, unable to separate from each other, the two men's shoulders touch: the photograph that symbolised their rivalry. At the time, I was happy to shoot Anquetil alone, in close-up, just for me, but with hindsight I should have liked to have taken the other one, the one where the two men have the whole width of the road just for them, but where the intensity of their effort pulls them together like a magnet, where each is leaning on the other's shoulder with expressions that chorus: this has got to stop, the pain is too great and the race too absurd.

So much has been said and written about that climb: that Poulidor should have attacked earlier, that Anquetil had found a better gear, that the gradient was too steep at this particular point, that Poupou could have followed Bahamontes who had broken away earlier if he had wanted to. Psychological domination has been mentioned, or a war of nerves. I don't believe it for a second. It's not at moments like this that one sets the psychological machinery in motion: you are simply stretched to the limit and you do your job, which is to get to the top of the mountain as quickly as possible on your bike. Poulidor and Anquetil are pumped up, they are twins, and each of them will know victory and defeat. Poulidor may have escaped Anquetil, but not by enough. Anquetil will have been dropped by Poulidor, but not by enough. As for me, I have my two photos.

I also come down from the mountain with a few further questions. Was Anquetil the most fantastic defender in the history of cycling? Had he perfected the most destructive way to push himself to the limit? To refuse to stay behind Poulidor, to use him as shelter, to want above everything else to stay level with him, to get his wheel in front; was that the proof of his greater strength?

Was this defeat – because that's what it was – the best way to ensure final victory in Paris?

When the photographs were developed in my attic on Rue Gambetta in Saint-Étienne, I stared at them for a long while. Poulidor could clearly be seen to be making a supreme athletic effort, at the limit of his strength and in the bright light of his profession as a racing cyclist. But Anquetil was as pale as a corpse, his eyes lost in a secret world that was not the world of the bike, drawing his strength from somewhere unreachable, from a well of mystery.

What Drives Anquetil?

As a young cyclist, I had clear ideas about what a champion should be. So clear that I wrote them down in a school notebook along with the photos I cut out of newspapers and stuck in according to a system that I'd invented. That notebook was both my pantheon and my commandments.

A champion was first and foremost someone driven by the desire to succeed, and to do that he had to love his sport above everything else: that was all there was to it. The achievement consisted in winning again, winning always, or losing in such a way that the defeat was a victory. Photo of Anquetil.

The second mark of a great cyclist was an unshakeable love of the bike. Alfredo Binda, who laid his bike in his bed and who slept on the floor if he thought he had performed badly, seemed to me the norm. I had his photo.

A great champion could also be recognised by his complete indifference to money – cyclists weren't footballers! To race and win enough to race some more seemed to me an enviable fate – it's true I had no idea of the terrible pangs of hunger, or of everyday needs. Photo of Walkowiak.

Like me, the true champion accepted pain as a given in his tough job. He tamed it until it became his ally, even when he was taking a rest, something I excelled at. Photo of Geminiani.

In this controlling of pain, the champion was a healthy being who could allow himself a banana during a race and a cream puff for Sunday lunch along with a Gauloise (but not inhale the smoke). He was allowed a strong cup of coffee before the start, and a big bottle of Perrier at the finish. Photo of Bobet.

A champion was a generous, modest person who withstood the low blows from his adversaries and from fate without a word, and knew how to recognise his opponents' merits. He should never hesitate to offer someone else a victory whenever he could. Second photo of Anquetil.

It goes without saying that when I was of an age to revisit these commandments in the light of my idol's career, I had to revise some of my judgements, and I even made some more discoveries ...

Is it achievements?

As far as achievements are concerned, no one has ever notched up more.

ANQUETIL: I saw what he was up to, the great Geminiani. At first it was a throwaway remark, nothing more, as if said casually: 'You know, whoever could win the Dauphiné and Bordeaux–Paris back-to-back would be in clover for twenty years! The public would kiss his feet! But it's only a dream ...' Then nothing more for weeks. I knew Geminiani through and through, so I let him stew it over.

When I had first thought of taking part in both races as I drew up my timetable of events at the start of the season, I realised they came one right after the other and that to do them both was impossible.

Geminiani came back to me a few weeks later on a different tack: 'You need to do something outstanding, to pep up your contracts for next year.' He knows that kind of argument works on me. I'm not against money, and I don't like to race for nothing.

Some time later, it was Janine who stoked the fire: 'He's crazy, Gem! What's this about racing both the Dauphiné and Bordeaux–Paris on the same day? It's impossible.'

So that's how the trap was laid, and how it became hard for me to refuse point-blank, laughing to myself.

They know I'll say 'nothing is impossible for Anquetil', and that I'll attempt it. I like gambling too much, and to make the bet myself rather than have others bet on me. Geminiani thinks he's a great psychologist. He is, but definitely not as great as he thinks. I know Janine well enough to guess that she told him I was now in his pocket, that she had worked on me. It's

true; I'm up for it. But it's also true that to take part in
these two races one after the other makes no sense unless
I win. It's not a matter of doing an eight-day race in the
mountains and then the longest classic of the year within
a few hours of each other, plus a transfer by plane with
no possibility of sleeping: I have to win them. Or at least
win the first one then see what happens in the second.
Only a madman would do it. Only Anquetil. Janine and
Gem are right: this kind of achievement gets noticed.
But Anquetil is the one who has to do the hard work.
Those two scheme, they chat, and then they watch me
pedalling away, thinking how right they were to push
me a little.

So I give in and take the lead: 'Have you sorted out
the details for the Bordeaux–Paris? We'll have to find
a plane.' Geminiani is beside himself: I've surrendered,
but then the trouble starts. Delighted, he announces the
feat out loud everywhere in the press, and when he is
loud, you can hear him a mile off. As soon as they hear
the news, the organisers of the Dauphiné are furious.
They send me a letter saying I am devaluing their race
by wanting to do another one immediately afterwards.
The public is going to end up thinking that their Alpine
outing is too easy … They have to be convinced it's not
so. So then, while Gem is sorting out the jet, I set out
on the Dauphiné. I have to take care of Poulidor, who
is determined to make his mark. I'm going to have to
play my cards right and count on the bonuses in the first
stages because when we get to the mountains, the terrain
favours him a lot.

At Saint-Étienne I come second behind Desmet and have gained a fifteen-second lead over Poulidor. At Chambéry I have a one-minute-fifteen-second advantage, but I struggled on the hills. I got dropped on the Col du Berthiand, and in the Revard I had to be an acrobat on the descents. I'm afraid of the Grenoble stage. As often happens in the Dauphiné, it's cold, and there's nothing worse than that. I put everything I've got into not losing time. I go past Kunde, I'm the one doing the hard work, and I don't let Poulidor get a wheel ahead of me, I stick to him like glue. The icy descent near Chamrousse is pure horror, I can't feel my fingers any more and I've forgotten my cape. All I need now is bronchitis. It takes me ages to warm up again. I come sixth, Poulidor seventh.

That animal has improved in time trials. On the penultimate stage in Romans, I have to really sweat: I only gain thirteen seconds on him over 38 kilometres, even though I'm not exactly taking it easy: my average speed is more than 44.5 kph. But the race is won; nothing more will happen now, and in the 220 kilometres to Avignon I have a rest at the back of the peloton and start to think about Bordeaux. Or, more exactly, about Paris, *via* Bordeaux. I can't wait to be in the Parc des Princes.

Then the strangest time trial I've ever had begins. Five o'clock: Finish line in Avignon. 17.05: Podium, kisses, bouquet of flowers. 17.10: Run behind my mechanic to the Ford Taunus – Gem is at the wheel, hold on to your hat. 17.20: At the hotel, bath, light massage, steak tartare, camembert, strawberry tart, a few beers. 'Can't you see Poulidor is quietly heading for the start as well … coming second in the Bordeaux–Paris is never such a bad thing either.'

17.55: Car again with the bikes on the roof and Rostollan beside me, speeding off once more, the motorcycle riders clear the way for us, we're driving at top speed. 18.30: Nîmes airport, interviews and massage in the waiting room. What's the weather like in Bordeaux? It's raining, thanks very much. 18.35: The plane is a Mystère 20, René Brigant is at the controls, and Gem tells me that it's De Gaulle himself who is lending it to us. I know this will be my one real chance to rest, so I raise my legs on my case, which I've put on the seat in front of me, and close my eyes for a second. The engines start to whine. We're hardly in the air before we're descending again. In Bordeaux, the panic of the transfer, getting the bikes ready, warm clothes for the night ride. Stablinski and Denson are there, ready to lend me a hand. I'll have to keep an eye on Simpson, who wants to win. My legs ache. I'm sleepy. Instead of going to bed, I have to race 557 kilometres. The first 258 of them all alone in the drenching night, and the rest flat out behind the trainers' dernies. At more than 50 kph. Madness.

At 1.30 in the morning, we plunge into the dark night, the road dimly lit by the cars following us. It's cold, and the north-west wind is against us. When it starts to rain again, I tell the photographer on a motorbike who has just taken a photo of me, like some nocturnal bird in a woollen bonnet, that I'm going to abandon. To do these two races back-to-back is simply impossible. Even those who have specially prepared just for the Bordeaux–Paris and are at the top of their form are suffering. I can see them. Even Simpson, who is a strong guy, even the inde-structible Stablinski, who looks out of it. Yet he's the one who tells me to keep going, it'll soon be dawn, and then everything will become clearer. Denson is pedalling ahead of me to keep up the pace and protect me from the wind. I carry on for a few more kilometres to please him, but I feel weak. How many dark questions can you ask yourself during a night spent racing in the rain when your legs hurt so badly?

At Châtellerault, before teaming up with the train-ers, we stop: a break for a pee, wash, undress, take off the jersey, a quick massage. And then, as I climb back on the bike, the abyss. The cyclist's abyss: you don't want to do it any more, you don't need to do it, it's not worth it, there's no point, they wouldn't treat animals like this, no longer to have to move, ever, especially not to pedal, at last sit in a warm car, not to be a racer any more, not to listen to them, to sleep, wear a suit, put on a tie, to be a regular guy, normal like all the others.

'Get out of here! Your place isn't in my car, it's in the broom wagon. Off you go! Get out! You're making me look like an idiot, me, Geminiani, for putting my trust in you! You're betraying me! Let me tell you something: it's all over between us! Shake my hand one last time … I should never have trusted a poof. Because that's all you are, Jacques, a poof and nothing more.'

At that moment, I really would have liked to be a poof, as he said. Or a different guy, it doesn't matter. To be anyone but me. Gem never held back: it's Stab who takes me by the hand and leads me to my bike. My leg rises of its own accord, without my permission, and bestrides the saddle. Then the first turns of the pedal in hell, the putt-putt-ing of the derny and big Jo Goutorbe is in front of me, ready to pull me along. He's piled on pullovers and jerseys to make himself even bigger, and pedals with his knees out to shelter me from the wind. His back is the only horizon I have, I can't see anything else, he'll have to deal with everything, I'm asleep as I pedal, I no longer exist.

It's pain that wakes me up. The sudden acceleration is brutal, going from 25 to 50 kilometres after a night of ankylosis is terrible. My legs are screaming, my back's on fire. But I recognise the pain: it's the one I know from my Friday training sessions, it's familiar, it's the Boucher pain, the memory of it comes back to every muscle, and paradoxically does me good. I'm suddenly hurting where I should be. Hurting where cyclists hurt. Goutorbe looks round to see how I'm doing then accelerates a little, to test me. I manage to keep up with him, and I'm back in the race. Denson is in the lead, as expected. But what wasn't expected is Mahé's strong attack. We'll have to reel him in calmly with Simpson and Stab. Not so calmly in fact, because now it's Simpson's turn to attack. Stablinski tries hard to get back on terms with him. I'm finding this sudden acceleration tough going, I catch up gradually, but I'm still on the edge of the abyss. The sun has come out from behind a cloud and we reach the foot of the hill at Dourdan – I recognise this familiar landscape and then, miraculously, I start to sweat. That's the sign: I've become a racing cyclist again. We pick up speed. Goutorbe doesn't turn around any more, he pulls me on. We catch Mahé. I leave Stab and Simpson to fight it out on the ups and downs of the Valley de Chevreuse, and in the Côte de Picardie I am Anquetil. At this pace, it will soon be me pushing the derny on. The road streams along beneath my stomach, my legs speed round, the gear whirls, my front wheel flirts with Goutorbe's back mudguard. He accelerates and we tip over the summit. He looks back, we've opened up a gap. Then the descent, the Sèvres bridge, the Porte de Saint-Cloud, the route de la Reine, the Parc des Princes, 57 seconds in the lead, 2,500 kilometres in nine days.

I'm surprised at the immense ovation I get from the public. Geminiani and Janine were right. Afterwards, the ceremony, the bouquet of flowers, the interviews, I admit to the journalists that I feel 'a bit weary'. If they only knew. We can keep my true sensations and my true feelings for later.

Is it love of the bike?

As far as love of the bike is concerned: 'room for improvement'.

'The bike isn't and never has been my greatest concern', Jacques would readily say in that mocking tone of his. If one insisted, he even added, without smiling: 'I really think that I don't, have never, and will never love the bike.'

He wasn't just being provocative with this kind of declaration: Anquetil no doubt did feel he was the prisoner of his bike. Being able to ride five kilometres an hour faster than every champion on the planet may bring in a fortune, but it also creates obligations and then it becomes quite difficult to make your bike a symbol of freedom. One can understand that climbing onto the beautiful machine is not a pleasure every morning. Especially as it brings suffering and because, even if the suffering is all inside, one can legitimately blame the bike.

Of course, it's the same for all cyclists everywhere, but as a general rule, out of regard for their beloved public, they choose the other face of the coin to express the secret wavering of their hearts: they show the positive, golden side of their relation to the profession. Anquetil, though, sees everything as black: either to provoke, or just to be different. As ever, his taste for adopting a pose and his mischievous understanding of the situation. If he says he loves his bike, no one will raise an eyebrow. If he confesses he detests it, the news flashes round the world … and yet I'm sure he does love it.

If people insist still further, he also confesses that the technical side bores him, and he is happy to leave it to the mechanics to choose his bike and gears. But it would be remarkable if he didn't cast an expert eye over his machines now and again. All the ones you can see in the photos or films are the latest, most technically advanced of their time: a Reynolds steel frame, aluminium rims, MAFAC centre-pull brakes, pedals with big flanges, headsets, Campagnolo cranks and derailleurs,

Pivo crossbar, Brooks saddle. Nothing is left to chance. Once he knows he has the best, Anquetil can afford to seem nonchalant. And yet, when it comes to beating the hour record, he's the one who demands the same frame as Coppi; when he has to struggle up the very steep gradient of La Forclaz, he's the one who asks Geminiani to find a way to get him a lighter bike.

When visiting kids are allowed into the garage of the Anquetil family residence, they're surprised to find at least twenty bikes, dozens of spares and a hundred or so tubulars drying for the next season.

After his career was over, Anquetil only got on his bike three times. Even then, people had to insist. On the last occasion, his daughter Sophie goes on at him: she has seen photos of him on his bike everywhere at home and in the newspapers, and now she'd like to see it for real. Anquetil resists. One day however, on her eighth birthday, he makes up his mind. The weather is fine, the table is set out by the swimming pool at Les Elfes, and as a special birthday treat Sophie sees her father heading straight for her, finally perched high on his lovely machine. He crosses the lawn majestically towards her, then plunges straight into the pool, still on his bike. This is to be the only time she sees him on it.

Is it money?

As far as money is concerned, things become complicated.

The young Anquetil is bending down. A boy among the girl pickers, he's picking strawberries and putting them in punnets. His back is bent the whole day: it teaches him to be supple. To complete his quota, he has to fill 50 boxes every day. He can also be seen in mid-air, shaking an apple tree. He earns the price of his future bike penny by penny. An Alcyon. His father treats him like every other worker, shows him no favours. Head down, he works.

At the little farm near Le Bourget that is his parents' home, pompom roses climb the red-brick front wall. One photo shows an adolescent Jacques, high up on a ladder, wearing jacket and hat, his nose deep in an enormous rose that half-hides his face. A pose like that of the mime artist Marcel Marceau, a dreamy, frail, Pierrot look that is the opposite of the tough guy of the pelotons. And yet there is nothing unfocused about his expression. 'I didn't pose for that photograph. I often used to pluck a flower. It was my way of looking over to the other side of the Seine, at the bourgeois homes, with their deck chairs on the lawns and boathouses.'

Anquetil knows what he wants. He dreams of a comfortable, bourgeois life, and to achieve it he starts out by being different. He styles his hair, he is well dressed, he wears black polo necks in order to stand out. He likes to hear it said of him: 'Anquetil is the kid dressed in black.' Although his family background is poor, he wants to be the most elegant, the most noticeable person around.

At the start of his cycling career, it's Roger Hassenforder, the rather crazy sprinter, who helps choose his ties. Later on, Janine selects his suits, the suits he dreamt of wearing every night during his races, instead of those ghastly tracksuits. Didn't he once, towards the end of his life, admit that in a dream world he would have liked to have been a transvestite? In the meantime, he wants to be rich. 'Obviously in me there is a desire to get ahead, the wish to climb higher in a society that had allotted me my place. When I saw that my first big victories brought a look of admiration to people's faces, and above all put money into my bank account, I told myself: if you want this to continue, make sure you don't become a fan of yourself. I've never been dazzled by myself; I always stayed no more than proud of what I've done.'

Victory is the shortest route to money, but not just any victory. When you are capable of winning everything, you have to avoid becoming overextended, boredom, and above all, unnecessary victories. An unnecessary victory is one that increases neither your reputation nor your earnings.

Back then, racing cyclists earned their living above all thanks to the criteriums organised in the summer after the Tour de France. Every small town and village wants to have its own race with that year's champions, wearing their lovely winners' jerseys. In general, these 'competitions' take place on a closed circuit where you have to pay an entrance fee. The spectators crowd in, and the organisers are willing to pay good money. The cyclists receive prizes based on the results and from sprints offering bonuses, which are given by local businesses in need of publicity. Most of what the riders earn, however, is from the appearance money, which they get whatever happens in the race, and which depends in large part on their fame. Two rival agents, Piel and Dousset, share out the cyclists and negotiate the best contracts for them. They also act as advisers to the competitors and can recommend different strategies throughout the season to increase their financial potential. They are both strategic and financial advisers. They can also have a negative impact on the outcome of races, as for example in the 1959 Tour, when the rivalry between them led to Henry Anglade losing the race. As one can easily imagine, their relations with the managers of the different teams is not always plain sailing.

Anquetil, of course, is the star attraction and pockets the largest sums of money. He is determined for this not only to continue but for it to increase. He does all he can to make sure that this happens. If his fees look like dropping because of an average season, he goes for the hour record. One more victory won't add anything to the cheque he receives? No matter, he'll win two.

For the criteriums, the cyclists are expected to put on a good show and to race properly, but things are made a bit easier for them. They ride short distances, on tight tracks known as 'tourniquets' so that the spectators can see them several times. In general, they use smaller gears than usual so as not to tire themselves out; above all, they decide the result in advance, or at least the general outlines of the race. Each of them is given a role to play. It is a spectacular performance designed to show off their jerseys. It's this routine and the slightly too obvious lack of a challenge that will soon mean these events cannot cope with the passage of time and the impact of television. In the 1960s, these criteriums are exactly like a regional theatre tour where everybody knows the play: someone from the region makes the first breakaway, the French champion catches him, then it's Poulidor who goes to the front, Darrigade reels him in, and in the end … it's Anquetil who wins. The show over, the circus moves on for the next start the following day. This is often several hundred kilometres away, and means a long night of driving. For the riders, this is harvest time, and they store their riches.

Anquetil is rich, and so it's easy to say of him that he has a cash register instead of a heart, especially since he is the first to declare to all and sundry that 'cycling is too hard to race for medals'. He buys chateaux, land, cattle, big cars; he has a beautiful, well-dressed wife, like a movie star, who is his driver. He's a star who's hard-headed in business. He argues passionately over his contracts, as much for the fun of it as for his love of money.

At one particular criterium, an organiser decides to pay him only half the agreed fee because he remained invisible in the middle of the pack and refused to put on a show. Anquetil accepts the penalty without a word, acknowledging that he didn't play the game properly. The next year, he wins the same criterium by a lap, and asks the organiser to pay him not only his fee, but also the half he is still owed from the previous year. And he gets paid.

Anquetil is rich and money also becomes a work tool. Not all of it is spent on chateaux and Ford Mustangs. Money serves to make more money; Anquetil is both champion *and* boss. He can afford to be. He is the best, he is without doubt the most intelligent, he is the highest paid, and money becomes one of his means of making sure that this lasts. At a certain point, the world of cycle racing seems stable: one knows what everyone else is worth, what they are capable of, what their right price is. For Anquetil, it's enough to know how to properly distribute victories, achievements and money among his team-mates and the other riders: to some extent, to pay a good rider a good price, and to continue to pedal like nobody else in order to be paid like only he is paid.

～

And then one day this stable arrangement comes crashing down. Something happens to drive the champion wild, make him lose his bearings; an incomprehensible phenomenon that escapes what he thought was the only logic possible in his life. And that phenomenon is called Raymond Poulidor.

Raymond Poulidor is a very good racer, a good climber, good on the flat, likely to get better still, but Anquetil immediately has the measure of him. Poulidor can test him, defy him, push him to the limit, but he'll never beat him. He hasn't the same toughness, and Anquetil immediately gains a psychological ascendancy over him. That's already a victory. The only problem is that the public is crazy about this rosy-cheeked peasant, this wise child who turns coming second into an honour. Without meaning to, Poupou has become, in the eyes of the public, a kind of positive opposite to Anquetil, and his eternal victim. By contrast, he makes the Norman rider look disdainful, arrogant – in a way Anquetil had never imagined, because he was too busy simply trying to race faster than everyone else. And since the public wants Poulidor, Poulidor wants to be paid the price of love. And Anquetil discovers that love can be worth as much, even more, than talent. He is furious, and realises too late that he has not trained for this kind of race. When it comes to the public's love, he's lost before he starts. He is somebody it's so easy to admire but so hard to love …

Worse still, the more he proves his excellence, demonstrates his superiority, the more he pedals like nobody else, the more popular Poulidor becomes. Anquetil is caught in a trap of pride that infuriates him. An even more devilish trap because Poulidor is a nice guy, someone he can be friends with, a mate playing cards, someone close to the land like him, someone who buys cattle. He doesn't bear him a grudge, because he knows that the real adversary isn't Poulidor, it's love.

The rivalry between them, stoked by the media, reaches its paroxysm, and then the devil of temptation raises his ugly head. This devil is Piel, Poulidor's manager, and the rival of Anquetil's man, Dousset. He's the one who pulls the strings, drives up the fees, and he has the key to the treasure chest: if Anquetil lets Poulidor win the next Tour de France, he promises it will send his market value through the roof. Fifty definite contracts each worth 50,000 francs, at the very least. A gold mine.

Anquetil thinks it over, weighs up the money and the glory, and for once decides he's not going to chase the money. He's going to ride to win. This may be the only time, but it's an important one.

Is it pain that drives him?

When it comes to pain, I was dealing with a specialist.

ANQUETIL: The Grand Prix des Nations demands a lot of training. When it was coming up, I often used to turn to M. Boucher, my first adviser. His moped was torture. Several weeks before the race, every other day, I trained in his slipstream. Nothing like it for tearing apart your muscles. The lowest speed: 40 kilometres an hour, and at times more than 60! Sometimes it was terrible. When it was hurting too much, I begged Boucher to slow down, but you don't know him: that only made him speed up! So I clenched my teeth. It's possibly thanks to that training that I never had to use up all my reserves of energy in a race. I pedalled to the limits of my strength in training; I learned to pace my efforts in the second half of a race, and to go flat out at the end without running the risk of cracking.

There's a huge difference between 'hurting' and 'hurting yourself'. Athletes are well aware of this. Anquetil doesn't like to hurt, but knows how to hurt himself more than anyone. This scenario is neither passive nor directly masochistic. In certain sports it's an essential part of the path to victory. In cycling, this *via dolorosa* is visible. Seeing a hundred-metre sprinter fly to victory in less than ten seconds only gives the outsider a faint idea of the pain he has suffered during his preparation. But seeing a cyclist struggle up the Col du Galibier gives a clear idea of his calvary. Those who endure a race and feel pain are suffering from the rhythm imposed by those who inflict pain on themselves. Anquetil belongs to this latter category. He has often said that he went to places filled with pain where only he ventured, but that he went there completely willingly.

To enjoy his power is pure enjoyment. For hours and on the most varied terrains, Anquetil could produce tremendous efforts that left ordinary riders standing. It was his thing. It was for him that the terrible thirteen-toothed gear was specially created – the absolute nuclear weapon for racers in the sixties. In 1967 he even risked using it on the track: the monstrous (at the time) 52 × 13 became the gear for his hour record. Back then people wondered how he could push it round without tearing his muscles and tendons ...

ANQUETIL: The peloton is out of control, nervous, you can feel the tensions, alliances being made. I'm afraid of a low blow. My team-mates are grumbling, my opponents are getting in a state. I take the lead right from the start. I need to put some distance between them and me. I shift into top gear and speed off. From then on I don't turn round, but keep accelerating. I don't ask anything of anyone, no relay, no helping hand. If anyone tries to come up alongside, I accelerate still more. That's how it's going to be until things quieten down. Behind me, the field becomes strung out, and I can sense that one by one the weaker riders are being dropped. There's not a sound any more. The peloton is having to work hard, and is suffering. I keep accelerating.

This reminds me of my first races as an amateur, when I knew nothing about bikes or racing. I simply rode at my own speed, and soon found myself alone, with nobody following me. Now it's the best cyclists in the world who are behind my wheels and are breaking their backs to keep up. We can do a hundred kilometres in hell if need be. I'll calm them down.

Is it drugs?

As for the healthy life, let's see.

Jacques Anquetil and Ercole Baldini, who have so often crossed swords, meet one year at the Grand Prix de Forli time trial. They're going to race one another yet again, they know the opposition, and know the race is theirs. They'll do the one-two, as cyclists say. All that's left to decide is who will be one and who will be two. A mere detail for them, who respect each other and no longer need a victory as such. The previous evening, over a dinner they share with a few friends, an idea occurs to them: 'Since we're certain of winning, why don't we do so on mineral water, just to see? We won't take any amphetamines, nothing.' They do the deal almost laughing, a bit of a joke.

The next day they race, as agreed, with no tablets, no injections. They win. Their average speed is a kilometre and a half less than that of previous years, the road seems endless to them, they have the impression they're dawdling along and suffering martyrdom. They meet at the finish, worn out. Anquetil was one, Baldini, two.

'We'll never do that again!'

'Never, I promise.'

⌒

Anquetil dopes himself and says so publicly in *L'Équipe* in 1967: 'You have to be an imbecile or a hypocrite to think that a professional cyclist who races 235 days a year can keep going without stimulants.'

A team-mate prepares everything in his metal box. The tablets, the injections. Amphetamines, always, to make the road bearable, to make the race more intense, to make the tarmac sparkle, to postpone pain and fatigue, to be able at last to pedal the way Sartre writes, to pedal the way the children will soon be dancing, forgetting themselves and the whole world, on a day free of aching legs when you feel just a bit stronger than yourself. To pedal on the edge of dreams.

The peloton dopes itself, and the peloton knows what is good for the peloton and always has done, because the peloton is the world. Outsiders will never understand that going slower is not an option, that to dope yourself is a decision as old as the invention of pain, and that doping is part of the history of mankind. Unlike taking drugs, it's not an individual decision, it is collective, and reflects their universe. Anquetil's is a nervous, jagged one: he loads his soul to free his body. The predictable damage is in the distant future, whereas the hill to climb is right there, straight in front of him.

When Anquetil repeats, in *France Dimanche,* that he takes drugs, everyone condemns him. His sin is being too frank. He ought to keep things hidden, play the game, lie. Everyone wants him to retract. But he makes things worse by saying that those who think you can be a racing cyclist without doping yourself are liars. He knows his buttocks have as many holes as a colander. But they're his buttocks.

Meanwhile, in full view of everyone, he fills his water bottle with stout, sugar and caffeine: one part drunkenness to two parts energy. Everything you might need to be a winner.

Later on, he'll even experiment with pastis, no doubt slipped into his bottle thanks to his triumphs in the Super Prestige Pernod. But all that is completely authorised by the anti-doping authorities.

ANQUETIL: In 1966, I was dreaming of a pure race, a race without a single blemish, a perfect victory or an equally perfect defeat. A race with no scheming, no skulduggery, a real bike race. It was to be Liège–Bastogne–Liège, the doyenne, the best of all. I asked my team-mates to hang back, to leave it to me, not to give me any help. The weather is hot, I feel good. I want to leave them all behind simply by pedalling: Altig, Merckx, Janssen, Motta. But above all it is Gimondi I want to test myself against: he has just won the Paris–Roubaix and the Paris–Brussels one after the other, so it's time to show him what's what. If the race follows its usual course, it will be on the climb at Wanne or on Mont Theux that I'll attack.

Genet, Spruyt and Schleck are out in front. They're only a minute ahead, and they're the sort one can catch: I'm riding alongside Motta, Merckx and Gimondi. Stablinski has pulled out due to mechanical failure on the climb at Wanne; at Theux I couldn't, in the end, get away because of the three up front. I didn't want them on my back wheel and then run the risk of getting beaten in the sprint finish at Liège. It was boiling hot, and heat is always on my side. I turn the screws during the climb and look around me. They don't look too good: Altig's feet hurt, he's constantly changing position; Eddy is lying too flat on his bike to be really on form, Motta will be the first to go, he's got that look about him. Which leaves Gimondi, who is as enigmatic and handsome as ever, pedalling easily. Now it's the climb at La Bouquette. Here we are. Without any violence, without pulling away, simply increasing the pressure, I accelerate. They become strung out behind me. I accelerate again. Merckx is beaten, Altig is left standing, Motta and Gimondi look at one another for a second too long to decide which of them is going to fill the gap I'm creating. Too late, I'm away. I accelerate again, reach the summit and then adopt my time-trial position on the bike. I'm alone, in my element, the world's best riders are behind me, I go for it. Now for the three breakaways. As soon as I see them in the distance, I know they've had it. I pass them going flat out to make sure they don't get any ideas about fastening on my back wheel. They don't react at all. I enter the outskirts of Liège. This is my pure race, my exemplary victory in the finest of all the classics – me, the rider of stage races …

On the podium, they all come up to congratulate me. They're experts, and know that I've 'done the job' as we cyclists say. 'There was nothing I could do', groans Gimondi. 'My thighs are exploding', says Altig.

The journalists crowd round and I'm overwhelmed with questions. Then this little, insignificant-looking guy pushes his way through and heads straight for me. As if he's joking, he tells me: 'Okay, Monsieur Anquetil, now you'll have to pee for us!' I won't do anything of the kind, my good man.

~

The next morning, all the newspapers praise Anquetil's achievement, declare that he is definitely the number one cyclist in the world, that his performance is unheard of. But the judicial machine is at work and the Belgian

Velocipede League disqualifies Anquetil, Altig and Durante for having avoided the obligatory drugs test. And so Jacques Anquetil will never add his greatest victory to the official list of honours in the Liège–Bastogne–Liège race.

'I know that rule was created in Belgium,' he says, 'but I challenged its validity and its usefulness right from the start! Apart from the fact that applying it in no way resolves the problems of doping, it is discriminatory and unpleasant for a professional cyclist. We are men, not horses, and it's our duty to combat this law, which offends our dignity and creates suspicion.'

Doping is a way of life that Anquetil never gives up. He will never renounce being the master of the day and the night, the master of intensity, the master of the beginning and end of all the parties. His daughter Sophie says that he even doped his goldfish. To see. It's also said that he encouraged his staff to stuff themselves with amphetamines so that they could work day and night, finish the harvest in record time and then all sit down at table together to devour the rest of their energy. Or so it's said.

Saint-Étienne is buzzing with a cycling rumour. A friend tells me: a race has been organised for under-twelves on the outskirts of town. 'An elimination race for mini-sprinters', he says. I don my Anquetil shirt, jump on my green steed, and find myself at the foot of a straight road climbing gently between two factories. The idea is to have the kids race each other in pairs over 400 metres. There's a line drawn in white chalk on the tarmac; that's the start. The same higher up: the finish. Each rider is given half the road (lengthwise) and woe betide anyone who strays over it into his neighbour's territory!

Anquetil isn't a climber or a sprinter, but he accepts the challenge. In the early rounds, he easily defeats not very tough opponents, then harder ones as the defeated riders return home. Anquetil reaches the quarter-final and wins. In the semis, he is wary of the big, strong opponent and has to fight right to the line in order to win by half a wheel. He's red in the face and puffing and panting (slightly overweight)? Now he's in the final without having time to get his breath back. He has a worthy rival: it's even whispered he'll be going to the Premier Pas Dunlop competition … Anquetil has drawn the right-hand side of the road; he avoids looking at his opponent so that he can concentrate completely on his race. He positions his front wheel on the starting line, raises his pedal for the off, and when the whistle blows launches himself, head down. The effort I make to get into gear is so great that my back wheel, pulled violently by the chain, works loose and jams against the bottom of the frame. The bike comes to a juddering halt, and Anquetil is thrown forward, his stomach slamming into the stem of the bike. It hurts. Furious, he punches the handlebars and watches as his jeering opponent, hands high on the handlebars, slowly completes the 400 metres of his triumph. Anquetil protests, makes an official complaint, demands a fresh start, shows them the mechanical failure. The winner looks at me disdainfully: 'You need to learn to tighten your wing nuts, little brat!' (Back then, I didn't have quick release.) Anquetil doesn't respond. He is going to have to give Pinza d'Oro a good telling-off.

Is it generosity?

Here, things become complicated.

At first glance, it looks as if, with Anquetil, calculation wins out over everything else, and his generosity is part of that. This is true up to a point. When Anquetil gives, it's because he has received, or he is counting on receiving something in return. One thing is for sure: he's no miser, still less with his money than with his strength (rightly or wrongly, all the observers place avarice in Poulidor's camp). He is one of the first riders in the Tour de France to give all his intermediate bonuses to his team-mates. He knows his overall victory will permit him to recover all that and more from the criteriums held after the Tour, and also knows that by doing this he is creating loyalties among his satisfied partners. Some of his talented team-mates earn a lot more in his service than if they raced for themselves. This kind of generosity, invented by Anquetil, became the rule: ever since then, all the yellow jerseys give their bonuses to their team.

Anquetil also knows how to impose his faithful band on the organisers of the lucrative post-Tour criteriums. They all want him and, in order to get him, are willing to agree to a few sacrifices by also taking his lieutenants.

There are also many examples of when he plays second fiddle to his team-mates so that they might add a victory to their trophy cabinet in an unimportant race: it's the best way for him to be sure of their complete loyalty when it comes to the bigger challenges.

The most emblematic example of this has to be that of the last stage in the 1961 Tour. Cazala has had a good race, and proved essential in the desperate defence of the yellow jersey that Anquetil has worn since the first evening. To celebrate the end of the Tour, the 'boss' decides to take him under his wing – or more precisely on his wheel – and leads him gently to the Parc des Princes. And there he allows him to win and enjoy the ovation that follows, as lord and master of the Park.

During his memorable Bordeaux–Paris in 1965, he is grateful towards the unexceptional Vincent Denson for the support he gave him during the most difficult moments in the night at the start of the race. He is so generous that Denson himself can't get over it: he's never won so much money on his bike.

Anquetil talks of the endless and often not very friendly arguments he had with his most talented team-mates, those who could have won more races (but not more money) if they hadn't been backing him up. He means Everaert and Novak in particular, who complained of being in his shadow and unable to show off their talent.

'Okay, it's true,' they would say, 'you are stronger than us, but what if you weren't there?'

'Then there'd be Gimondi, Motta, Merckx ...

I'm like Johnny Hallyday or Adamo, and you are my orchestra.'

He also knows how to be generous with his worthiest opponents. When, during the 1966 Giro, Motta, who is in the lead, asks him not to make life hard for him on the final stages, he accepts. At the top of the Tourmalet, Jan Janssen, the yellow jersey, doesn't feel at his best. He catches up with Jacques: 'Monsieur Anquetil, *piano* if you please', and Jacques slows down. In Turin, when Lucien Aimar takes the yellow jersey, Anquetil embraces him – to everyone's stupefaction, Aimar above all …

When it's his team-mates, the sharing is clear. But with his rivals, this generosity is more complex and ambiguous. Occasionally, the orchestra sounds out of tune. 'Yes,' he confesses, 'I've bought riders.'

A man, a victory, a helping hand, an entire team – they can all be bought. Is it in return for money that the Pelforth team helps him on the descent from Envalira in 1964, enabling him to catch that morning's breakaways? Is it in return for money that in the last, bloody stage of the 1966 Paris–Nice, the Italians get behind Anquetil while the Peugeot team takes sides with Poulidor? When a team or a rider has no more chance of winning, why wouldn't they be for sale?

Anquetil doubtless remembered the story that Coppi told him some years earlier: during a race that he wanted to add to his honours ('at any cost', one might say) he was a long way in the lead together with a nobody from the peloton who stuck to his calves like a leech. Whenever Coppi accelerated, the other man did as well, and the *campionissimo* began to be worried. Discreetly, he offered him 1,000 to let him win. The lad did not reply, but pushed even harder on his pedals. 2,000? Nothing. 3,000? 4,000? Coppi thought the youngster must be feeling very strong. 5,000? The other rider only just managed to nod in agreement before collapsing exhausted into the gutter.

Often, while I was contemplating my plastic peloton, I was worried. Worried that Anquetil might not win. He wasn't very reassuring. He didn't give the impression of solidity and seriousness of someone like Bobet (who at first I called Zonbobet, because of his first name, Louis). When I talked bikes with my father, I had to admit that he wasn't such a good climber as Charly Gaul. I was a thousand miles away from understanding that the slowness with which he saved his energy on the climbs was due to a scientific approach and his own self-knowledge. A way of protecting himself from the aggression of pure climbers. I should have so liked Anquetil to catch Charly and leave him for dead, to teach him not to escape like that under his nose when the climbs started. I was a novice at cycling strategy, and Anquetil annoyed me. His provocations made me shudder. 'What's he up to now?'

I would ask myself. I was afraid he would be put in jail, or thrown out of the peloton. My father shrugged his shoulders, doubtful.

What does the public expect from a cyclist in the early 1960s? What little Paul himself expected of them in his schoolbook: first and foremost a cyclist must be a worker, more a worker than a boss. Money must never be his chief concern: he earns very little, and the few who do earn a lot are generous enough to conceal the fact. A cyclist must suffer. Ever since Albert Londres' articles from the 1920s, he is a 'galley slave of the road', and it has to cost him. No slackers in the peloton. No moaning either; there's no rain that's too icy, no wind too disruptive, no mountain too high: at the slightest complaint, the cyclist is threatened with being sent to push skips deep in the mines. A cyclist must always promise to do better the next time, and without artificial help. Following Pélissier's confessions, we know that cyclists dope themselves, but the public won't accept it: the champions don't dope themselves because they are champions, and the others don't dope themselves because they only came second. During a race, a cyclist has to be noble, a good winner and a good loser. He respects his rival, and knows that the price of victory is hard work. In cycling, the best man wins. By pedalling. For the public, cycling is revenge against life's injustices.

Anquetil is a spoilsport. Most cyclists play the game, out of stupidity or habit, self-interest or conviction. He insists on telling the truth as he sees it. He's going to tell it loud and clear, and that will mean people detest him even more. Of course, since Anquetil is Anquetil, this truth will shake and stir everything, and professional cycling will never be the same again. There is a before and an after Anquetil, and each of his declarations creates a small revolution in the peloton.

Robert Chapatte, former racer and budding journalist, and as astute in his second career as in the first, asks Anquetil if he would agree to race for medals. Where any ordinary rider would speak of glory, of different jerseys, would dream aloud of an Olympic medal (cycling wasn't yet an Olympic sport in those days), Anquetil grows angry. A cold anger of the sort he is so good at. He restrains himself, and replies calmly: 'The Grand Prix des Nations is now worth a million old francs to the winner. If I still raced in it, which is possible, and if I won it yet again, it would take me a little over two hours, which means 80,000 old francs a minute. Just so you know, with a 52 × 14 gear (which is the one I usually chose for the Grand Prix des Nations), that means one revolution every 7.8 metres, so that each turn of the pedal brings in a 1,000 old franc note.'

This miser's calculation exploded like a bomb. So all Anquetil wants is money! We thought he only cared about glory and panache, but here he is counting every turn of the pedal! He's not a true racer, he's a cash register!

'It seemed to me completely crazy, if not downright stupid, to go and struggle on a bike for nothing, just to be proud that you go faster than somebody else. Occasionally riders smashed themselves to a pulp in devastating crashes … Yes, I thought they were stupid, and had no wish to play the fool on the roads with them.'

In 1967, at the time of the Tour de France, he speaks his mind in four articles for *France Dimanche*. They all have very provocative journalistic headlines: 'Why I don't like Poulidor'; 'Yes, I doped myself'; 'Anquetil Accuses' (about the death of his friend Tom Simpson); and 'Yes, I've Bought Riders'. Some of them are accompanied by very striking images. All the rules are broken: respect for your opponent, the anti-doping crusade, respect for the organisers, the transparency of sporting challenges … After they appeared, there is such a scandal that Anquetil has to adopt a low profile, and even go into hiding at one point. He's thrown the toy out of the pram, and the peloton is scared stiff and won't get over it. It will do so, and the questions remain unanswered, but at least Anquetil asked them. He would have been mad with himself if he hadn't.

ANQUETIL: There's no point beating about the bush. The hardest, most terrifying race for a Frenchman is the Giro d'Italia. I was the first Frenchman to win it. But I have to humbly confess that without a rock-solid team I would never have finished that year. And if I didn't win my last Giro, it's because I couldn't get together enough money to buy a team at the last moment. When I started the 1967 Giro, I had a complete team with excellent riders like Stablinski, Novak, Lemeteyer, Den Hartog. We were racing for the Bic team. Ten riders might seem plenty. But, believe me, that's the minimum number for the Giro, because we were ten against a hundred and fifty. Without counting everyone else. The *tifosi* who give the Italians a helping push, and pull their rivals back by the jersey, spectators shouting insults at you from the roadside, people spitting in your face. In cycling you hear a lot about the 'Hell of the North', but for me, hell is the Giro. So much advertising money is poured into it that it's absolutely vital that an Italian wins. Italian TV can't be objective either: if a foreigner is in the lead, a third fewer viewers watch the finishes. So anything goes: backward pushes, screens of riders forcing you to take risks to overtake them, kamikaze riders coming straight at you to force you into a ditch, or even a ravine. It's impossible to win a race like that without team-mates.

～

One summer's day in the middle of the Tour de France, I go out for a ride with two mates. One of them will be Roger Rivière, the other Raymond Poulidor. I'm Jacques Anquetil. We planned to do a 24-kilometre circuit, but all three of us know that the real test for the champions will be during the terrible climb at L'Écorchée, which rises above Aurec-sur-Loire. A winding, three-kilometre ascent with an initial steep slope, where only real experts can make a difference. From the outset, Anquetil makes a typical road racer's attack. He accelerates powerfully, but makes the mistake of taking the second bend on the inside, where the slope is steepest, and he is passed on the outside by Poulidor and Rivière. Head down on his green machine, he concentrates, eyes fixed on his front wheel in a maximum effort. He sweats, pants, but can't rejoin the two breakaways. At the top he comes third behind Rivière, who is first, and Poulidor, second. I'm furious with myself for making Anquetil lose. If only that climb had been ten kilometres longer, I'd have shown them. I am disgusted with myself and sulk. From now on, I'll dedicate myself to solo efforts. I'm furious.

Anquetil is annoying

Anquetil is annoying in every way: if you accept that the great champions are naturally endowed with great willpower and a taste for hard work that gives them a few seconds' advantage over the best of their rivals and a good handful over the peloton in general, the use they make of this varies widely from one champion to another. Merckx, for example, pays cash for those seconds: he's the strongest and he makes sure everyone knows it straightaway, all the time, everywhere. That's reassuring for his admirers. Armstrong concentrates his advantage on one or two races a year, and on one or two strategic moments within those races – the moments that pay: time trials and arriving at the summits. The rest of the time, he controls the race. He is economical, calculating, strong and cold. Those who admire him say he keeps his promises. For his part, Bernard Hinault regulates his minutes like an artist of racing. He can choose to demonstrate his superiority anywhere, at any time:

there are no special points in a race, and any moment can become a hell if he so decides. The shape of a stage becomes what he wants, what he creates. That makes him one of the finest creators in the history of cycling. As for Anquetil, he's annoying. He uses his trump cards irrationally (that's why Poulidor always beats him at cards), he's not interested in the race, he frustrates his team-mates, he lets huge possibilities escape.

In 1963, the course for the World Championship isn't very hilly, but its length and the violence of the attacks have spread the field out. Only the strongest are out front. A few kilometres from the line, Anquetil pulls away from the peloton, flattens himself still further on his bike, slips into his highest gear and rides like a pursuit cyclist; he's using those few seconds' advantage he has over his rivals. Now's the moment. The pack can't gain a metre on him. All of a sudden, against all sporting logic, he turns to look over his shoulder. He sees the peloton spread across the road, flying along, and says to himself that he won't make it, he can't keep it up. This is a beginner's mistake, because every cyclist knows that in a situation like that, you don't look back, you go for it. He sits up, is caught a few hundred metres from the line as the sprinters take up their positions. Tom Simpson starts things off with a strong push to Van Looy's back (that kind of thing was common in those days – the TV didn't yet point a finger at anyone). Van Looy takes the young Beheyt on his wheel. They sweep across the road from right to left, blocking Darrigade as they do so, and on the line it's Beheyt who dares beat the Emperor of Herentals by a short wheel's length. Van Looy, who thought he was going to be world champion for a third time, is hopping mad. In the changing rooms, only Anquetil dares approach him. Only champions can face the tantrums of other champions. 'I pay him!' shouts Van Looy. 'I pay him and he dares to beat me!' Anquetil tries to calm him down, but there's nothing doing. Van Looy is beside himself. He punches the shower wall in his fury. 'Why didn't you win it? Why did you sit up a kilometre out? We were all going as fast as we could, but couldn't take a metre off you. Why? You should have gone on. It would have been normal for you to win.'

~⁓⁓

Anquetil is annoying: he expects always to be offered the honours corresponding to his position. In 1954, at the start of the Grand Prix des Nations, he senses that something strange is going on behind his back: the mechanics look away, people give him evasive answers. He suddenly discovers that Francis Pélissier, his trainer at the time, has decided to follow Hugo Koblet rather than him during the race. The support car is useful in case there's a mechanical problem or to give time checks and encouragement at difficult points on the route. Anquetil is to have his mechanic Jacquot on his tail. He's furious. For Pélissier to follow Koblet seems to him like high treason. Pélissier's complete trust is as precious as the little tricks he knows how to employ to give his rider an invisible helping hand when necessary. A slight acceleration when the rider takes on food or drink and is leaning on the car door for a moment, for example, the brief shelter he can give going round a corner, the shout of encouragement to help him step up the pace ...

To Anquetil, this defection has the effect of a whiplash. So he decides to gallop. By kilometre 25, he's ten seconds in the lead. By the 39th kilometre, it's 25, and by Rambouillet, it's four minutes! He turns around and sees the maroon-coloured muzzle of Pélissier's Hotchkiss catching him up at full speed, and finally falling in behind him, where he should be.

After crossing the finish line, Anquetil's anger hasn't fallen. The race record has. Koblet comes nowhere. Anquetil rejects Pélissier's congratulations and rounds on him in no uncertain terms.

That evening, Anquetil sends his winner's bouquet to Mme Pélissier, who declares: 'He's a strange boy, you never know what he's thinking.' Oh, really?

~

Anquetil is annoying because he knows perfectly well how to make sure he loses. The 1958 Paris–Roubaix race is a stunning proof of that. It's a long, difficult course, with dangers because of the cobbled sections, its dips and hills, the uncertain weather, the dust, the mud, the north winds. To beat Van Looy and his 'red guard' you have to have everything going for you. That Sunday, Anquetil's legs feel strong and he has a plan: he'll attack early to give himself a margin before they hit the cobbles. He speeds off at kilometre 70 and is out front with seventeen other riders, among them friends like André Darrigade, Jean Stablinski and Jean Bobet, who won't refuse to help if need be. Since he's fresh, he goes flat out for long stretches, and little by little drops his rivals, but also his best partners, and finds himself on his own with two Belgians who have no interest in helping him. Without the support of those he hasn't been able to give a helping hand to, he begins to lose time. The peloton comes back to one minute fifteen seconds. Then bad luck strikes: he punctures when his safety margin is already too narrow. At the cost of a rather desperate effort, he hits the front again, but he is exhausted and is caught by the bunch four kilometres from the velodrome. Seventy riders enter the track together for the sprint, and Anquetil pulls back: he's not one for mass sprints. Van Daele wins. Anquetil's conclusion is more one of anger than analysis: 'One-day races are a lottery, I'm not interested in them any more.' He never takes part in Paris–Roubaix again. In 1981, Bernard Hinault makes sure he wins it in style before declaring loud and clear that this lottery race is 'a load of crap'.

This doesn't prevent Anquetil from having a few later regrets. In 1973, during the same Paris–Roubaix race, he is a TV expert, and is following Merckx in a press car. Merckx is out on his own and is speeding to victory. Then he skids on the slippery cobbles, falls, gets up and sets off again. Anquetil leans forward and confides to the journalist in front: 'You see, he at least did what I didn't manage to do in 1958. He gave himself a proper safety margin. He was no slouch in his effort, he didn't calculate with a slide rule. If I'd done the same, I would have added Paris–Roubaix to my list of honours.'

When things aren't going to plan, Anquetil also knows how to throw the losing machine into gear. In the 1959 Tour, victory seems likely to fall on Henry Anglade, that mean-spirited, authoritarian little Napoleon riding for a regional team who has taken the lead under the prestigious noses of Anquetil and Rivière. Anything but that! The idea that a French nonentity can steal a march on the two great rivals of their time is simply unbearable. Especially as he has chosen as his manager Piel, the arch-rival of Dousset, who is their manager ...

It's raining stair rods and the course is formidable: the cols of La Madeleine, L'Iseran and the Grand Saint-Bernard, the highest and coldest on the way to Aoste. The great Bobet himself has climbed in agony and then abandoned his bike for ever on this rooftop of the Tour, on the summit of L'Iseran, an immense champion finally beaten by pain. Forgetting this warning sign, a group is up front and has left the climbers behind. Among them are Anglade, Gérard Saint, Anquetil and Rivière. In the valley, it becomes obvious that these last two are hanging back and refusing to do any pulling. Each one blames the other: 'He's the one who doesn't want to race...' In fact, they have secretly got together and are slowing the breakaway as much as they can to allow Federico Bahamontes, the Eagle of Toledo, to catch up. They see him as a much worthier victor than this young Anglade fellow.

No one is taken in, and when the Tour arrives at the Parc des Princes in Paris, Anquetil is roundly booed. Back in Normandy, he buys himself a boat to sail on the Seine and names it *Boos 59,* his own way of attending to his popularity.

⌒

Anquetil is annoying because when he gets an idea in his head, he pursues it to the limit, whatever the cost. In 1961, he wants to fulfil his dream of winning the Tour de France wearing the yellow jersey from start to finish. This is a huge challenge, because it's not his style to defend. That way of riding implies constant vigilance, a taste for keeping the whole race in your head, keeping an eye on what all the others are up to: none of which are Anquetil's way of doing things. So above all, this is a challenge to himself. A test.

He makes sure that he has a good, loyal team around him, and they all set to work with the same goal. Anquetil attacks from the time trial on the first day, and opens up a lead of three minutes on everyone else. From then on, the team's mission is to keep everything sewn up. At the end of a few stages, the press and the organisers start to complain: they would much prefer a race with lots of changes and drama. They get it on the stage to Chalon-sur-Saône, where a breakaway group gains seventeen minutes on the peloton. The general classification is set to explode! Then Anquetil, refusing all help, does what in cycling jargon is known as a 'job': he takes over at the front of the peloton and stays there for 30 kilometres. Behind him, it's panic stations: the riders can't keep up the pace and are dropped one by one. Anquetil reels in the breakaways, makes up the seventeen minutes and keeps his yellow jersey. In the Alps, where the climbers are expected to react, a heavy fall by Charly Gaul spoils things, and Anquetil keeps his jersey. When they reach the Pyrenees, all the observers are hoping for a tough battle, but Charly Gaul seems resigned: 'I tried to drop Anquetil ten times,' he explains, 'and ten times he simply increased the pace. I can't get away from him, I "telegraph" my attacks. I've grown old!' The Pyrenees are a flop as well, and Jacques Goddet, the race director, is furious: 'He ruined all the climbs by setting the pace up front and no one wanted to challenge him.' As a final insult, he calls Anquetil and his rivals 'dwarfs of the road'. Antoine Blondin prefers to say that his friend Anquetil is the 'manager of the road' ... Anquetil wins the next time trial, and then, having achieved what he set out to achieve, he offers the last stage to his team-mate Cazala by keeping him on his wheel right up to the Parc des Princes ...

And finally, Anquetil is annoying because he's lucky. One can also measure champions by the opposition they have to beat, and although Anquetil had worthy opponents throughout his career, you can't say that he was confronted by another champion as great as he was.

His career took place between the ageing Bobet and the young Merckx. He did, however, have to face some very great specialists: even past his best, Bahamontes was a formidable climber, but he was no good on the descents and never managed to raise his game in the time trials. Charly Gaul was in some senses the opposite of Anquetil. He climbed like a climber, with fearsome attacks; he loved the rain and deluges, but if he was unbeatable on a steep climb or during a tough mountain stage, he found it hard to go the distance in a Tour. For his part, Van Looy was an exceptional champion, but he did not compete on the same terrain, because his weakness in the mountains meant that he was more suited to the one day-races that Anquetil scorned: he was a model to adopt, but he was beatable. Ercole Baldini and the sculpted Rudi Altig were the only ones who could get near Anquetil, and even beat him, in solo races, but they had their limits in the high mountains and didn't climb as well as he could. That leaves Poulidor. He was without a doubt the most complete rival, the most capable of winning, and yet he lacked the terrible soul and true complexity of a champion.

For his first Tour de France in 1957, Anquetil has the benefit of a very unusual set of circumstances. Confident of his power, he has let it be known that he prefers to race for a regional team with his friend Darrigade rather than alongside Bobet in the French national team. The two men don't like each other much, and the idea of supporting one another in the race doesn't exactly appeal to them. Then suddenly it's high drama: Bobet, tired from a strength-sapping Giro, decides he isn't going to do the Tour de France. His withdrawal dismays many people. But the door is ajar and the young Anquetil knows how to push it wide open. Roger Walkowiak, who won the previous Tour thanks to a bit of luck, cannot impose himself as a natural leader. So Anquetil finds himself in command, with a team in top form ready to give their all on every kind of terrain. It's baking hot, and as early as the second stage Charly Gaul, his most formidable opponent, the one who could have stolen the high mountain stages from him, abandons the race. Between Besançon and Thonon-les-Bains it's the turn of Bahamontes, the Eagle of Toledo, who regularly leaves him behind on the climbs, to sit down at the roadside and give up without any further explanation. They beg him to get back in the saddle – for his mother, he refuses, for his wife, he refuses, for Spain, he refuses, for Franco, he still refuses. He stays kicking his heels and waits for the storm to pass. His manager, Luis Puig, finally gives in and Federico climbs aboard the broom wagon … The road is now clear, and Anquetil can do his thing without fear of the great climbers. The French team plays the game and despite a scare in the Aubisque, at the age of 23 Anquetil wins his first Tour de France.

Similarly, 1960 is another example of his luck. All of a sudden, he's on his own: Bobet and Geminiani retire; the promising Gérard Saint is killed in a car crash and, above all, Roger Rivière falls during the descent from the Col du Perjuret, breaks his back, and never gets up again. He would have provided the stiffest opposition to Anquetil: the world hour record holder, Rivière was an exceptional racer on the flat who was also perfectly capable of conquering mountains. He was also destined to win the Tour de France, but Anquetil did not have him as a rival for long.

～

The second time I saw Anquetil, I didn't see him; I tracked him down. My father and I followed his bike tracks. This was in 1961; I was fourteen, and the previous year he had given such an apocalyptic account of his climb to the Col de Gavia in the Giro that my father had immediately decided that we had to do it as well, just to see. Anquetil had described a mule track cut out of the muddy earth in the mountainside, not made-up and with no barrier, a place for skidding and vertigo. He had described what it was like in the rain, transformed by the elements into a dangerous stream of mud, with the rock wall on one side and the abyss on the other. He had described the blasted *tifosi* who pushed Gastone Nencini up as hard as they could, and who, their feet stuck in the mud, showered him with threats and insults. The journalists who knew this apocalyptic region had added that there were bears roaming the area ... This was more than enough to whet my father's cyclist appetite; more than enough for me, the following summer, after a painstaking approach by car, to get on my bike and follow him. I climb, fortunately in dry weather, up 20 kilometres of dirt track until we reach an altitude of 2,618 metres, struggling with the sand and pebbles that made my back wheel skid, and the incredible gradient (22 per cent!) of this goat trail, my face covered in dust, my throat parched, pedalling my way to the Great Jacques' Revenge. I may have bust a gut, but as a consolation and to my immense relief, I have to confess I didn't see any bears. A link was forged with Anquetil thanks to our shared effort. We were closer, I had matured, and the time had come to probe other mysteries. If Anquetil was passionate about solitude, he was no longer alone. From now on, I was with him, and I discovered that there were lots more people around him ...

Odd Couples, Strange Band

'As soon as I cross the frontiers of the small circle of my friends, all human contact miscarries', says Jacques Anquetil. For her part, Janine tells us: 'He couldn't stay alone.' We're faced with a paradox emphasised by Jean Bobet: 'There will always be something strange in Jacques Anquetil's miraculous life, something that renders him inaccessible to everyone: opponents, the public and doubtless even to friends.'

I'd have liked to be Anquetil's friend. He'd have laid his hand on my head and given me a cap, a signed photo. He'd have taken me for a ride astride his bike, in his arms. He'd have given me his yellow jersey and gone off towards his hotel, naked to the waist, half of him tanned, waddling like a duck. My friend Anquetil.

I'd also have been friends with Mme Anquetil, but I would have used the 'vous' form of verbs to be polite and would have taken naps on the back seat of her Mercedes during the long boring hours of the stages on the flat.

Janine is the driver

Janine, known as Nanou, came into Anquetil's life like a door slamming. She was the wife of his best friend, his mentor, his doctor, Doctor Boëda, from Rouen. She had two children, a girl and a boy, was seven years older than him (she admitted to two), and she didn't like him. This fair-haired, stuck-up kid who attached himself to her home got on her nerves. Her children, Annie and Alain, on the other hand, adored him and wanted to follow him and accompany him everywhere, like a kind of brilliant elder brother.

He was there, hanging about the house, getting in his hosts' way, doubtless getting in his own way. Visible rather than attractive, no doubt closer to the doctor and the children than to Janine. It's even said that Janine advised the doctor to pay more attention to his patients than to this fair-haired cyclist.

Then, one day on holiday in the south of France, Janine, on her own with the children, invites Jacques, who is visiting them, to go out with her one evening. He accepts, then pulls out, because he has been invited elsewhere and prefers this new offer. When he arrives at his function, he discovers … Janine. It could have ended with a slap, a cutting remark, a sulk. But on the contrary: they spend the evening together, leave together, pressed up close to one another, never to part. Sometime later, Janine runs away from her husband's house wearing only her nightdress, in a rented truck. The heartbreaks begin, love clings on. It's made of stainless steel.

For the young Anquetil, Janine is a trophy and a godsend.

Janine is a former athlete: she knows, she can guess. She had also been a nurse, which perhaps also explains it. She weighs her champion in the balance of love but also in that of his talent and his uniqueness. He's not a cyclist like the others, he won't be a man like the others, but she knows how to accompany him in victory, to direct him without forcing him; she is lovingly certain of that. 'She needs my victories as much as I do. I'm not only her husband, I'm her champion', Jacques says. And he adds: 'At first, she even wanted them too much.' Did she want to do the racing? If she had, who would have driven? I am personally grateful to Mme Anquetil for having perfected such a great champion for us.

They make a formidable couple. Anquetil pushes Janine in everywhere. He admits that it's not always easy with his managers and the other cyclists. The peloton likes to keep women at a distance: they're said to cause trouble, there's no room for them in this all-male clique. The prejudice is deep-rooted, and Anquetil has to fight tooth and nail to make room for Janine. He refuses to give way and, since he is Anquetil, Janine will triumph. She imposes herself in his world thanks to her beauty and self-assurance. She looks like Martine Carol, dresses fashionably; her photo is soon in all the magazines. She is asked for her opinions and advice. She has tamed the lion.

Jacques publicly acknowledges that he owes her a great deal. 'She has given me a fresh taste for victory. She has that amazing power.'

Janine anchors Jacques in his gift. She doesn't try to oppose the feelings of doubt or revolt he has towards the bike. That would be catastrophic. Instead she channels it, analyses it, understands it and gets the best out of it. Utterly devoted to Jacques, she is secretly on the side of the bike.

～

To be a cyclist's wife and to want that role one hundred per cent means accepting being on the road. Janine always drove. First the Chambord, then the Mercedes, the Mustang, maybe the Thunderbird: she was always the one at the wheel. Their love was automobile. Nanou wasn't the kind to sit waiting for the return of her road sailor. She wanted to share the champion's life to the full. Good money was a question of kilometres for the criteriums, travelling night and day; a minute standing still could be expensive. From race to race, some 80,000 kilometres under her belt in the two months after the Tour – at 100 kilometres an hour, with the precision of the French railways. 'We live on the roads, at night. The car becomes our home. I sleep in it. I eat in it: usually sandwiches and peaches. Janine loads up kilos of them every day, and off we go, real cycling nomads.'

But Jacques sleeps sitting up. He has learned to sleep like that because he has heart problems if he stretches out. He goes over the next day's race, the menu for his evening meal, cherishes his dream of becoming a farmer, and then a chateau owner. He is not exactly thinking of the money. Janine takes care of that too. She is the one who, during the race, goes and collects the envelope stuffed with banknotes from the organiser – the one for Jacques (usually the fattest) but also those of the others, the friends, Stablinski, Altig, even sometimes those of his opponents. Janine watches over him, she drives, she counts, she accompanies. She also creates the spectacle. In one photo you can see her, magnificent in white shorts, lending Jacques her knee so that he can sign an autograph or contract more comfortably; she is his office, his muse. Their couple is so perfected it's indivisible. They only move apart when Jacques has to race.

The Tour of Spain, 1962. Janine stayed at home, but very soon she'll have to start driving, her love is always automobile. Altig and Stablinski have broken two forks: now there are only two spares for the whole team, and that's not a lot. The water bottles the Spanish organisers have given them leak (oh, yes!). The team has no caps or tubulars and, worst of all, Jacques has no more *demi-sel* butter or his beloved gingerbread. A phone call, and Janine is on the road. She loads up the provisions, fills the car at Rouen, and crosses France from north to south that night, and then Spain ...

Here is what Stablinski, Jacques' team-mate, says of her: 'Janine, his wife, is a character as well. She is almost as tireless at the wheel as Jacques is on his bike. During the races, she was an extraordinary organiser, packing and unpacking the suitcases, finding the good hotels and restaurants, and making us keep to our timetables, which is essential. She likes Genia (Mme Stablinski) a lot, but by the end of three or four days of that kind of life Genia was begging for mercy … and asked to go home.'

If need be, to be able to drive further, Janine dopes herself with Corydrane. Just like her husband, she wipes away the road and the night.

The feat has been accomplished: the diabolical double of the Dauphiné Libéré and Bordeaux–Paris is behind him. The public in the Parc des Princes has given Jacques an ovation. He's been handed his second bouquet of flowers in twenty-four hours. He's been interviewed, congratulated. He has thanked all the women and the men, winked knowingly at Geminiani, pleased at his ruse, and now he's in his car. He's crying out of tiredness, out of sheer joy, because for the first time he felt love passing between himself and the Parc des Princes public. A new feeling, one that he finds strange despite himself. 'I have the impression I've done something important', he confides to Janine between sobs. Soon his head droops and he falls asleep. He's lost the rhythm of sleep for two days and nights now. His body is shattered. Around the car, darkness devours the landscape; another hour to Rouen, and Janine is still driving.

Another early season Friday: in front of her, Janine can see the car's bonnet, the Mercedes star shining on the tip, almost impaling Jacques' buttocks. He is pedalling in front this time. He wants to have the wind blowing directly at him and for the car to push him on faster. Janine's foot on the accelerator is so sensitive that she knows exactly how to make the base of his spine hurt. If he slows at all, she'll crush him.

On another occasion, Jacques is behind the boot, protected from the wind. Janine accelerates to 50 kilometres per hour and Jacques follows. If there's any danger, he has only love to help him contact her. In the cockpit she has love too, but also demands, and her acute sense of Anquetil's pace. She's going to make it hurt him in the way he needs to be hurt to progress.

Even if he has trained well, she is frightened. 'I don't like the waiting, I fled from the Ford team hotel. I can't stay close to Jacques before the start of a time trial, it's beyond me. I call it the "vigil". A moment of unbearable tension. I feel as if everything is shifting inside him. He can't stay still, he worries about everything, his bike, the sky and the wind, which can change from one minute to the next. Besides, this time trial doesn't exactly inspire him. It's a course made to measure for Poulidor, and Jacques is sure to be beaten.'

Jacques is grateful. He knows exactly how much he owes his wife. He says it: 'I would never have got out of a driver all she has done and put up with: 100,000 kilometres a year, stages averaging 500 kilometres, she planned our itineraries impeccably, never any mistake, never late, she has always brought me safe into port.'

Occasionally, as well, now she is famous, Janine drives on her own behalf. Along the routes of the Tour, she becomes the ambassador for a perfume, an eau de toilette, a fashion label. She is beautiful, the magazines trust her, and she has understood perfectly the impact the world of cycling can have on non-sporting brands. The days when La Perle cycles competed with Bianchi bikes are well and truly in the past. The cyclists (and their companions) have become ambassadors for glamour and chic.

$\backsim$

And Janine always carries the cases. She could not bear it if something Jacques needs should go missing.

Whenever Jacques is racing, Janine sleeps. Most often in her car seat, sometimes in a hotel bedroom. Half an hour before the finish, she wakes up to go and collect the money from the organisers and to applaud.

The worst moment of the year for her is the Tour de France: three weeks when she doesn't drive, but stays shut up in her house, transistor to her ear. She blesses the rest days whenever there is one. Then she can cross the country to join Jacques in his break and spend the day with him.

The lieutenant

It took me a long while to add Jean Stablinski to my plastic peloton, and I was wrong. Despite the countless different colour jerseys he won, Stab always seemed invisible to me, as if he always won by slipping past the champions, taking them by surprise. He seemed a bit like the miners I used to meet in town: black-faced, shadowy. I had trouble seeing that he was red-hot.

$\backsim$

Jean Stablinski is a free rider. Free in his movements, free in his speech. He is quick, hard-headed, he knows how to win. He is so free he can perfectly well put himself at the service of a leader when his spirit of freedom tells him to. He is a professional rider who counts and knows how to count. Anquetil looks enviously at the world champion jersey he has adopted for a year to make a change from the countless ones he has won as champion of France. He's a formidable one-day race specialist.

On his bike, he has the invisible elegance of the canny: small, discreet, secretive even, he rides in your shadow then bursts past you at the very moment you can't take it. You could swear he is inside your legs and knows exactly when you're going to suffer.

He likes and admires Anquetil wholeheartedly, and with good reason: 'Working for a leader like Jacques Anquetil is both a pleasure and a guarantee of profit.' He doesn't mince words either when he paints a rare portrait of the person for whom he was the most brilliant, the most devoted and the least faithful lieutenant. He deserves to be heard. According to Stablinski, if Anquetil meanders along at the back of the peloton, it's not because he doesn't care, it's because he has the power to get back to the front when he decides to. According to him, Anquetil never has anything negative to say about his team-mates, even when they are asking for it, like Pierrot Everaert so often did. According to him, if Anquetil occasionally isn't interested in leading from the front, it's because he trusts his team-mates. Lastly, according to him, Anquetil is a comfortable leader because, if there is really too much going on up front, he is able to take the lead, accelerating hard and restoring order, to the great relief of his team. The portrait he paints of the rider is lucid; the one he paints in a few words of the man is subtle: 'He's not such an easy guy in ordinary life. He worries far more than one thinks. He only relaxes after the battle, not before it.' He insists that Jacques' supposed dietary excesses are part of the race. It's psychological warfare: the lobster thermidor he eats is a weapon against his opponents on a diet and is manna from heaven for the journalists.

Anquetil often plays the role of a mysterious character, and even when he isn't playing it, he remains a character of mystery. For Stablinski, it's easy to strike a balance on a professional level. Personal relations with the man are more surprising and difficult. 'Jacques doesn't make friends easily', he explains, 'but when he does, it becomes exclusive. You always have to be with him. His friendship is demanding, and sometimes intolerant.' This troubles him. But there were so many who knocked on the door of the Master's closed circle, those who wanted to be part of the clan. For his part, Stab finds this too much, and wants to keep a certain freedom. Too much intimacy could be a risk: Jacques could be an uncomfortable friend. He spoke little, and with little emotion; he could often tease. With him, the conversation was often not on solid ground, and you didn't know exactly where he was coming from. He often had a slightly mocking air that kept others at a distance. He could also be crude at times. Jean Bobet, an intellectual in the peloton who had a degree in English that should have turned him into a teacher, tells me that one day he was fed up with it, caught Anquetil up, and said to him: Stop saying "it's a load of shit" the whole time, it's not polite.'

Anquetil was such a mixture of self-assurance and doubt, of certainty and torment that he was very hard to comprehend. The whole world was supposed to admire him, and to achieve that he performed many admirable feats, but there were very few allowed to enter his intimate circle. Those who were chosen knew they belonged to a privileged world, a kind of court, and they quickly accepted the demands of friendship with Jacques because such friendships were strong and doled out so sparingly.

Anquetil is afraid of mobs and crowds. Something inside him is steadfastly timid, something is profoundly solitary. And yet he is described as loyal, generous, trusting. But always exclusive. Too much so probably, because from early on he's the leader of the pack, the centre of a closed microcosm. It's the miracle of Jacques Anquetil's legs that allows a small band of journalists, cyclists, followers, old friends, to be arrogant and even scornful when they wish to. Seen from outside, the Anquetil clan is quite frightening. Those not allowed into it readily ascribe to it evil machinations, mafia-style behaviour. His old mates find this comforting, with good meals and an air of trust; they share the success of their old friend. The journalists in the inner circle get a few scoops, and some go into business with him; the riders in his band know they'll be well treated. Jacques, though, pedals on and seems to want to allot each one a particular place, a function. Sometimes, he's the only one who knows what that is; at other times, it's obvious. It depends. There can be rows, tensions, splits among the little group, but at the centre of the relationship Jacques offers a generosity and a loyalty that often goes back to childhood and which he never betrays. For their part, his friends still gather round his tomb every November. That says something.

The different members of this band influence Jacques in different ways. Some of them are friends to have fun with, companions for a night out. Others, however, are real fellow travellers. Among them are two men whom Anquetil truly shared part of his destiny with. Two men who decided his life and his choices, as Janine did in other areas. Two men who pushed him from behind, and not merely literally. What Janine did out of love, these two others did out of friendship – which didn't harm their own interests either. These two men are obviously very different to one another, and the relationship they had with Jacques was paradoxical. Nothing to be astonished about there.

Darrigade

Sometimes I would play at scaring myself, to tell myself suddenly that I no longer liked Anquetil. Instead, I immediately liked Darrigade. It even happened sometimes, when I liked Anquetil with all my heart, that I also liked Darrigade, especially when my friends and I had sprint races. During our rides, each time we were drawing near a village, one of us would shout: 'Road sign!' and the sprint would start. The first to reach the sign won the right to laugh at the others. On those occasions, in top secret, I am Darrigade.

~⌒

It has to be said that Dédé Darrigade is a solar racer. Blond, blue-eyed, sinewy as a cat, as much a gambler as a winner. He's five years older than Anquetil, but he's the same generation. He embodies the youth and cycling devil-may-care attitude that Anquetil has: 'We were boys together.' He's the model of the joyous years, the easy victories, the bachelor triumphs.

When Anquetil arrived in the peloton, Darrigade immediately spotted him. He saw his talent, his gift, his insolence, but also the carefree attitude. The lack of seriousness in the approach, the lack of tactics in the battle. Since he himself is a very great champion, he recognises genius when he sees it, because there is also room for admiration in the peloton. Darrigade decides he will quietly offer the young Anquetil the ballast he needs to live up to his promise. 'Besides,' he says, 'he talks very little and I talk a huge amount, so we got on immediately.'

Anquetil has nothing to fear from Darrigade as a racer. Their talents are strictly complementary. Put together, they would have made the greatest cyclist of all time. Dédé's talent shines in the last 500 metres of a race, the part that Anquetil detests. The 500 metres of greatest risk, which are also those where most of the honours are won. Dédé belongs to the caste of sprinters. Anquetil admires all he has won: 22 stages in the Tour de France, world champion in 1959, the list of his victories is as long as your arm. In the last section of the race he is irresistible. Everyone admires him for the way he 'rubs', the way he slips into the tiniest gap in the middle of the peloton, his ability to read the race like nobody else. He's a master sprinter, a master road racer. He only hits his limit in time trials and the steepest climbs. He will never win one of the great Tours. The flat stages are his true realm, where Anquetil never had any intention of reigning.

So Darrigade took Anquetil under his wing without any ulterior motive. He became his friend, his route master, his mentor, his tormentor. He's the one who berates and scolds him before sharing his parties, his feasts, rooming with him.

Their friendship is based on a hearty appetite and total trust in the race. Together, they are both racing cyclists and kids. From the outset, Darrigade has decided to be Jacques' professional conscience. He needed one. How often did he go to the back of the peloton to exhort him to do his job? In the 1957 Tour, just when a big battle had started, he even lost him for a moment: Anquetil was not to be found, even at the very back of the bunch. In fact, he had got off his bike in an orchard and was picking peaches …

One evening, the Tour stops at Rheims. Darrigade has won the stage in the sprint. While he is waving his bouquet and smiling at the ladies and giving the journalists some quotes, Anquetil heads for their hotel. It's one of those provincial hotels with flowery wallpaper and striped bedspreads. Their window looks out over a square where passers-by are relaxing. As so often, in the room there's a double bed and a single one. Anquetil puts down his case and settles on the big one for a bit of rest before his shower and massage. Darrigade, who is sharing with him, arrives a moment later in his yellow jersey. He glances round the room, and complains:

'Oh, no! You always take the double bed. It's not fair.'

'Why isn't it fair?'

'You always take it. Why not me? It's my turn.'

'If you'd got here first, which bed would you have chosen?'

'The single one.'

'You see …'

That was how their duo worked. A few years later they fell in love at the same time. A few more years, and they got married. Their relationship grew more distant. Later, when Jacques became ill, Darrigade made fresh alliances. Later still, he changed teams. Life separated them, but their friendship remained and lasted far longer than cycling did.

Geminiani

Time passes quickly in the peloton, and generations follow one another at the speed of a sprint. The rising generation has to struggle against the generation that's already risen and that tries its best to make sure nothing changes. This rivalry is an established fact that goes way beyond any possible friendships between the two groups. Anquetil cannot be on an equal footing with Bobet, who is ten years older than him. He can only oppose him if he wants his share of the cake; and besides, he doesn't really like him. Nor can Anquetil be friends with Geminiani, whom he does like and with whom he shares a taste for the good life. They're not of the same generation and so are *de facto* adversaries.

✦

Why does Anquetil feel so distant from Geminiani? Unlike Darrigade, who is his ideal complement, Gem is his antithesis.

Stan Ockers' victory at the 1955 World Championship continues to rile Anquetil. Although he had opened up a gap at the front, he saw Ockers and Geminiani coming back on his heels, and he isn't sure if his teammate in the French team didn't favour the Belgian, who won in the end ...

Gem was to Bobet what Darrigade was to Anquetil, and to Anquetil's mind that also goes against him. Geminiani was never submissive, but he gave Bobet some of the greatest helping hands of his career, as well as some of the most spectacular dressing-downs, as a proud, independent lieutenant.

✦

As a child, Geminiani frightened me. Even though his Clermont accent sounded familiar (he was a kind of neighbour) his loud voice and trenchant opinions did not fit my idea of the discreetness that a true champion should have. Besides, he was known as The Big Gun, and all that was far too loud for my little ears. Everything about him suggested the hunt and prey. You always saw him sprint away, firing off and in my opinion not winning often enough.

I should have paid him all my attention however, because, off his bike, Geminiani is a great storyteller. He can recount a race like no one else; he always has a few anecdotes to add, he has verve and humour. He's a godsend to journalists, whom he provides with an endless supply of information, even if it's not always objective or trustworthy.

Anquetil is suspicious of him. He finds him too talkative, too tricky, too blustering; he's seen him pull too many stunts. He fears his scheming, his low blows. In 1958 Anquetil, who the previous year won the Tour de France, tells the selectors straight out that he'll have either Bobet or Geminiani in the French team, but not the two of them together: 'They're too crafty, they'd play some kind of trick on me.'

The two men stare at each other for a long time like bookends. Their cycling styles are diametrically opposed: where Anquetil goes for elegance, Geminiani is all swagger and pulling faces. The way they talk is the opposite as well: Anquetil is discreet, dry and ironic; Geminiani is expansive, unstoppable, funny.

But Geminiani is also a brilliant, imaginative businessman. As early as 1953, he creates his own make of bike. After his retirement in 1960, he changes direction and opens a brasserie-hotel in Place de Jaude in Clermont-Ferrand. But that's not enough for him: he doesn't want to leave the peloton completely, and so has decided to become a manager and, above all, Jacques Anquetil's manager. 'Sharing a table with Geminiani is one thing. But I don't want him as my manager. I still have too vivid a memory of him as a racer and all the tricks he played on us.' Anquetil tries to push Mickey Wiegant as director of the St Raphaël-Helyett team that's just been formed. But among his team-mates he's in the minority, and so has to make do with Gem.

⌒

As the months and races go by, as they travel, share dinners and parties, a quite odd trust grows up between the two of them. Geminiani, often praised for his solidity, finds he can influence the mysterious, the subtle Anquetil. He's understood some of what makes the champion tick, and is able to use this to good effect. With Anquetil he pulls on huge psychological strings that seem to work. He knows how to use his taste for the unusual, his need to be different, to be unique. He's perfectly aware of his taste for money, for profitable glory, and knows how to find the sometimes crude words to push him on. It's hard to imagine that Anquetil, with his powers of analysis and subtle temperament, takes all these remarks and orders too seriously or at face value, but he knows how to use them himself, doubtless whispering what he wants to Gem so that Gem can be the one to say them out loud. Or he is simply glad that somebody is betting on him, pushing him, keeping him centre stage.

On many of these psychological points, Gem finds a trusty ally in Janine. She knows how to steer Jacques, she knows that Gem does, too, and so they often join forces. Jacques can't have been fooled, but he benefits from it. He can see what they're up to, and doubtless is amused by it, doubtless trusts them, and definitely uses it to his advantage.

As Anquetil's manager, Gem doesn't go in for half measures. In the 1963 Tour, the riders have to climb the extremely difficult Col de la Forclaz before they reach Chamonix. Anquetil has reconnoitred it during a trip to the region and knows it's an awful climb. He asks for a very small gear (42 × 26: the use of 26 teeth at the rear was a rarity in those days). He is also dreaming of being able to use his ultra-light mountain bike, one made for climbing but not for descents. As the finish is after the summit, without any real descent, it would be ideal for that machine. But the Tour regulations ban any change of bike. No problem: Geminiani has decided to hoodwink the race marshal travelling in his car who is in charge of seeing that the rules are obeyed. At the right moment, Anquetil pulls up and shouts: 'Shit! My derailleur!' His mechanic jumps out and stealthily cuts the gear cable with his pincers. Geminiani shouts to the official: 'Shit, his derailleur has snapped!' The ultra-light bike is brought down from the roof of the car, Anquetil has set off again, and the official is invited to inspect the damage. Anquetil pursues Bahamontes, catches him and beats him in the sprint at Chamonix. In his long career, Gem has learnt a lot of tricks.

In those days, the world of cycling wasn't the exclusive domain of doctors (however demoniacal). There was a whole host of more or less shady 'healers' around the cyclists, pushing their magic potions and supernatural powers. Geminiani knew them well. Antonin Magne himself, the old sorcerer among sorcerers, didn't think it odd to hold his pendant over Poulidor's stomach to predict a difficult July. Cyclists have to make such tremendous efforts, and the stress of races is so great, that they cannot pass up the chance of any magic. 'What if it works?'

There's no doubt that for Anquetil 'it works'. Janine is categorical: 'Jacques is superstitious. Before the start of a Tour, he always wanted to see his healer. Without him he felt handicapped.' His favourite is Jean-Louis Noyès. His wife is a fortune-teller and he says he's a healer and magnetiser.

In 1960, before the start of the Criterium des As, a track race behind a trainer, Anquetil doesn't feel well. He hasn't slept for two nights, has a sore throat, and feels

an angina coming on. He's pallid and off colour. He calls
Noyès, who comes running and lays his hands on his
neck right under the starting tape. Jacques takes up the
story: 'On the seventh lap, I wanted to see if I could use
the thirteen-teeth gear. I accelerated and felt so good that
I never again had to ask Goutorbe my trainer to slow
down.' At more than 54 kph, he beats the course record.

This trust in mysterious powers could turn against
him. In 1964, Anquetil literally allows himself to be
invaded. At first he was scornful about an article that
appeared in *France-Soir* signed by a certain clairvoyant
by the name of Belline, announcing that he would dis-
appear during the climb up Envalira in the Pyrenees.
According to this clairvoyant, the thirteenth day of his
fifth Tour de France would be fatal for him. With Geminiani, Anquetil shrugged his shoulders at this, but as the
fateful day approached he felt vaguely uneasy, and then
began to take the threat more and more seriously. He is
frightened.

To take his mind off it, on the evening of the thirteenth day – a rest day on the Tour – he decides to bar-
becue a whole lamb with his wife and Geminiani. When
his opponents get to hear of this, they reckon he'll be
hung over the next day, and be slow to start, and so they
organise an attack.

Only a few minutes after the start of the stage, on
the climb up the Col d'Envalira, everything kicks off.
Anquetil is dropped by the peloton, and only has Rostollan to help him. He can't keep up with Poulidor or Bahamontes, who are flying. Then a terrible fog descends on

the road, and Anquetil is overwhelmed: the clairvoyant's prediction is going to come true. He trembles and goes even slower, on the verge of abandoning. The faithful Rostollan is obliged to encourage him and push him on. Anquetil is a shadow of himself.

Geminiani grows alarmed and organises a double riposte: he pulls alongside him, hands him a water bottle filled with champagne, and says: 'If you're going to die, you might as well die in the lead.' That's all it takes to banish the fear of the prediction. Anquetil crosses the summit, rides as hard as he can through the fog, blindly following the red lights of the cars in front of him. He catches Janssen and Anglade and then the breakaways before the finish in Toulouse, thanks to a welcome helping hand from the Pelforth team, who pull him along on the flat. Anquetil is alive, Anquetil is a winner. Geminiani is his sorcerer.

～

This taste for the supernatural did not prevent him from seeing the future clearly. Together with Geminiani, Anquetil brings a decisive change to the habits of the peloton, laying the foundations for a new kind of cycling. They are the ones who succeed in insisting on teams based on brands rather than national and regional ones. They bring sponsors from outside the world of cycling into the sport. At first it's the aptly named St Raphaël aperitif that begins to finance the team Geminiani manages; later on it will be Ford.

This is a huge change, because it paves the way for building homogenous teams around a leader chosen to achieve objectives decided on in advance. Van Looy was a precursor with his famous 'red guard', his Faema-Saeco team financed by Italian coffee-machine makers. They ruled the peloton, and made sure that they launched the authoritarian Emperor of Herentals into orbit.

Ultimately, Anquetil and Geminiani make one of the most remarkable duos in the history of cycle racing. The path they share is strewn with challenges, battles, lots of fun, hard knocks, big financial deals and a few memorable stays in hotels. They even pair each other in the Monte Carlo Rally in a Ford Mustang. And in the end, this amounts to an outstanding list of honours. Without Gem, Jacques' career would be far less brilliant.

Poulidor

Then there's the completely exceptional case of his great rival, Raymond Poulidor. Poulidor is Anquetil's luck; Anquetil is Poulidor's luck. They don't know it yet, and it will take them a long time to accept it.

I had no right to like Poulidor. You couldn't like Poulidor *and* Anquetil. That was impossible. And anyway, Poulidor and I were too similar: brown-haired, square-faced, with big jaws. We reeked of the Massif Central – him to the west, me to the east. We came from the same soil, and that meant we couldn't like each other. To everyone else, Poulidor was immediately and obviously 'Poupou', the darling of France, its teddy bear. It's difficult to think of a good nickname for Anquetil: 'Master Jacques' and 'The Great Jacques' as he was sometimes called, are more for the initiated than for the public. To the vast majority, Anquetil's name becomes anything from 'Anctil' to 'Anqueutileu'. It makes his name hard to pronounce, but it's not an affectionate nickname. Anquetil does not inspire that kind of affection. Like his friend Marcel Amont, one is tempted to call him 'Monsieur'.

The duel between Anquetil and Poulidor is first and foremost a battle between two ideas of cycling. A traditional idea, embodied by Poupou and his mentor Antonin Magne – an old-fashioned idea in grey smock and Basque beret – and a modern idea embodied by Anquetil and Geminiani, a Ford Mustang idea with the failings and surprising qualities of novelty and invention. Even though he is two years younger, Poulidor pedals old. M. Magne's methods are visibly growing rusty, and his race decisions are often catastrophic.

Right from the start, Anquetil has assigned Poulidor his place. He has recognised at once that he is a worthy rival, but he has put it into his head that he will always come second, and so he did. Anquetil's psychological ascendancy over Poulidor is a mystery one can only corroborate. Poulidor admires Anquetil, he watches the Caravel glide by, and this admiration is fatal for him. He's like a goalkeeper who admires a great centre forward: the fraction of a second's lack of attention due to admiration, and it's too late.

So it's been written that Poulidor always had bad luck. He punctures at the wrong moment, falls in a bad spot, is knocked down by a motorbike on his way to victory. All of this is true, but he also does his best to harm himself. He commits mistakes that are unforgivable at this level of competition and tension.

In the 1964 Paris–Nice, during the Corsican stages, Poulidor does an amazing 'job' on the climb up the extremely difficult Col de Teghime. He leaves Anquetil more than two minutes behind, and plunges into the descent, sure of winning. On a dangerous bend, he falls without seriously injuring himself, but wrecks his bike. This on a day when Antonin Magne has decided to follow Jean-Claude Annaert with the spare bikes ... Poulidor is left sitting on the roadside waiting for the replacement, and watches the race pass him by. When you know how Anquetil behaved towards Pélissier when he chose to follow Koblet rather than him in the Grand Prix des Nations, you can imagine the strip he would have torn off Antonin Magne. But Poulidor, ever the gentleman, waits by the roadside and lets everyone go by ... It is details of this kind that sometimes decide victory.

In the Toulouse stage of the Tour de France, it's Poupou's mechanic who pushes him too hard after a wheel change and knocks him over! Raymond quickly gets back onto his bike, only to realise that his chain has come off. Two minutes 30 seconds lost …

Managing these chance factors becomes part of a profession which, from that point on – thanks to Jacques Anquetil – is aiming at different goals, following different rules. Poulidor needs to know that, in the cycling of his time, even if not every low blow is permitted, certain ones are. He has a whining side to him that exasperates Anquetil fans but delights his own. They say there's a conspiracy and that their champion is only beaten thanks to the underhand means his rival has cooked up. And yet Poulidor's problem remains even when Anquetil isn't there. In 1965, Anquetil doesn't race the Tour, which makes Poulidor the favourite. Even so, he manages to lose to Gimondi, a 23-year-old substitute who has been called in at the last minute. Not only that, but he loses to him in every facet of the race, at Rouen, at Roubaix, but also in the time trial on Mont Revard. With their idol soundly beaten, the Poulidor fans find the real reason for his failure: it's Anquetil himself who wanted Gimondi to win, and the proof is that he invited him to dinner on the evening of the Rouen stage! Pull the other one.

This craziness isn't only on his side. The obsession with Poulidor can be grotesque on Anquetil's side as well. In the 1964 Giro, Jacques realises one evening that the lad ahead of him in the general classification is an Italian called Polidori. He says to Novak, his route master: 'Natole, have you seen the name of the geezer in front of me? Polidori. That's almost Poulidor! They're going to laugh at me in France. We've got to make sure that kid doesn't get anywhere.' And so the whole of the French team sets out to neutralise the poor Polidori, a modest second string who doesn't understand what's happening to him. As soon as he tries to make any move all the Frenchmen swarm round him. 'Anquetil knows very well I can't win the Giro! What's got into him?' In an odd reversal, during a transition stage Anquetil does something unusual for him. He starts chatting to someone in the peloton. 'He's a good guy', he tells one of his team-mates. 'What's his name?' Of course, it was Polidori, and that marks the end of the hostilities. The Italian only had to suffer from the Anquetil-Poulidor rivalry for a few days.

~⁓

This rivalry quickly goes beyond the two men. It no longer belongs to them, but becomes a matter for the press and the fans who have taken it up. No one can talk about Anquetil without talking about Poulidor. When Anquetil wins the Tour of Sardinia, which Poulidor does not race in, the newspapers hardly mention the victory but make headlines of the next confrontation between the two men. This infuriates Anquetil.

The battle rages at its fiercest during the Paris–Nice 1966. In the first stages, Poulidor takes it easy, claiming he is out of condition, but when they reach Corsica, he lands a blow by beating Anquetil in the time trial between Bastia and L'Île-Rousse. He takes 36 seconds from him, which is no mean feat. Anquetil is furious at being beaten in his speciality, furious at the reception Poupou receives from the Corsican fans, furious at having, he believes, lost this Paris–Nice that was meant for him. He's in a rage, and even Janine has to keep her distance. He ruminates, delves into his memories, consults old press cuttings. He has noticed that, following a huge effort, Poulidor pays for it 48 hours afterwards. He calls Geminiani and tells him he won't bother in the next stage, but on the last one, on the mainland, he will launch an attack. Gem needs to prepare the troops and their allies, because it will be total warfare.

This stage from Antibes to Nice has become the stuff of all the low accusations made of cycling in those days. Anquetil's team-mates attack one after the other from the first kilometre. It soon becomes obvious that the Italian Salvarini and Molteni teams are riding for Anquetil. At the same time, it's plain that the Peugeot riders are on Poulidor's side. One of them, Zimmermann, pushes Poulidor up a climb, and it's said that the motorbikes pull Anquetil up the climb at Tourette. Some of the cyclists claim to have been pushed into the gutter. Everywhere there are claims of dangerous riding, intimidation.

Adorni attacks strongly, and Anquetil lets Poulidor fill the hole on his own. Once he's done it, Anquetil immediately attacks, according to him 'fifteen, twenty, thirty times'. According to Poulidor, it's three times. But the thirtieth or the third is successful. Poulidor is exhausted and can't react quickly enough. Anquetil is away. He puts on one of those performances only he knows how to, alone in front of the peloton, riding as if it was a time trial, livid with rage. He beats Poulidor by one minute 30 seconds on the Promenade des Anglais and wins what seemed to be a lost Paris–Nice *in extremis*.

Their battle continues in front of the TV cameras. Poulidor complains bitterly that Anquetil rules the peloton, that he manages races and that his team-mates never miss a chance to behave badly. Anquetil responds that Poulidor is a poor loser, and that his interview isn't worthy of a true champion.

In the following Tour de France, Poupou is made a fool of once more. Anquetil is no longer at the top of his form, but Geminiani announces loud and clear that he will win everything. Poulidor plans his race around him, and makes him his only adversary. Meanwhile, Gem plays his joker, Lucien Aimar, and has him win the Tour under Poupou's nose.

The World Championship at the end of the season that year proves utterly counter-productive. The two men, who on that day are far better than the rest, find themselves alone on the last lap. One of them is bound to be world champion. When it's the bell for the last kilometre, they suddenly slow up. Poulidor doesn't want to go into a sprint with Anquetil because he knows he'll lose. For his part, Anquetil glances at Poulidor out of the corner of his eye, fearing a sudden attack on the slight hill in front of them. They glance at each other. They slow down. They watch one another. They dare one another ... and Rudi Altig, who can't believe his luck, passes them with 300 metres to go. Anquetil comes second, Poulidor third, and both are happy to have lost. Neither of them will ever be world champions.

'I've come to wonder if we're still in our right minds: the world of cycling, the fans, Poulidor and me. I think the way France is divided into two sporting clans is absurd, and so is all this passion, these threats. Haven't I even received anonymous letters with death threats?' writes Anquetil.

'I've found myself detesting Anquetil', is Poulidor's version of events.

⌒

Having reached these grotesque summits, this fatal pair were bound to end in tears or to fall laughing into one another's arms. Which they did. Anquetil even admitted that he was 'in a state of dependence with regard to Poulidor'. Their ridiculous battles having considerably added to their glory, not to mention their purses, they decided they were both winners and opted for a respectful and long-lasting friendship, based on late nights, nocturnal poker games and discussions as farmers. Doubtless in the peloton they talked cows: the Normandy breed with their big udders, the sure-footed Limousin ones. Until they ran out of breath. They were two incarnations of the old France linked to the earth; every race meant a new piece of land, an animal. They were not from the same region: the soil here is heavier than there, but they were from the same kind of agriculture, that of lords of the manor and peasants. They finally came to recognise this. In 1974, when Anquetil had become a selector for the French team, he made sure he chose his friend Raymond, who yet again came second, behind Eddie Merckx this time. Tough luck.

Legend even has it that on his deathbed Anquetil said: 'Poor Raymond, so I'm going ahead of you. Yet again, you're going to come second.' Asked if this tale was true, Poulidor said modestly that his memory wasn't that good but if by any chance it wasn't true, it perfectly well could have been: Anquetil was capable of making fun of him to his dying breath. But at that moment Poulidor was probably in no mood to laugh. It was a real friend he was losing.

~⌒

The third time I saw Anquetil for real was on the Col d'Izoard, just at the exit from the lunar Casse Déserte, where the road starts to climb steeply again after a short descent. I had climbed it in the sunshine that same morning, on my father's wheel. We had taken the valley of the River Guil, which serves as a step towards the col, then turned left at the famous crossroads with its sign indicating 'Col d'Izoard: 15km'. At last I was there, on that terrible climb where the history of the Tour was written. For a few kilometres I was slightly surprised: the climb wasn't that dreadful after all, and I could even climb it without shifting into my lowest gear. It was a moment of happiness, mingled with slight unease. Had my father deceived me about how difficult the climb was? Was this really the expected moment of truth? We passed Arvieux at a good pace and reached that long straight line at the end of which there's a village. My father told me it was called Brunissard, then said nothing more. As we progressed along the road, I could feel my legs growing heavier and see the handlebars rising towards my nose. I shifted into the lowest gear, but my legs were still leaden. Nothing on this straight indicated an incline, and so I couldn't understand this sudden loss of form. I had run into the invisible wall of Izoard. My gear was too big, I didn't have the strength, the road was too steep, the sun too hot, my water bottle too empty, my father was too far ahead of me (at least five lengths), the life of a cyclist was too hard, and I was too small.

Then we entered the forest and the trees wrapped their gentle arms around me. The road was still climbing, but now I no longer noticed it. With each hairpin bend I could measure the distance we had come and the altitude gained. Cyclists caught us up, the elegant tip of a banana dangling out of their pockets. They encouraged us, offered their full water bottles, gave us a push as they went by. Life became cyclable once more, and by strength of will I reached the famous right turn where my father was waiting for me, a broad grin on his face. I turned right and all of a sudden discovered the moon and a descent, which was a lot at one and the same time. The landscape was plucked bare: it was all scree and boulders, in every shade of grey, beige and brown, majestically sad, desolately sublime. I had never seen anything like it, and savoured it all the more because the road, in the middle of its ascent, had the good grace to descend for 500 metres to give a cyclist the time to enjoy its beauty. I couldn't get over it.

We took up our positions down below, where the road turns left, and waited four hours for the riders to appear, listening to their progress on a neighbour's transistor radio as the voice of Fernand Choisel crackled in the silence of the mountain.

Anquetil went past in a flash in a leading group that was climbing very quickly. He caught my eye because he was the only one who kept his position as a rouleur among climbers, who were dancing on the pedals. It was a tiny instant. The riders sped past the plaque in honour of Fausto Coppi, then disappeared round the right-hand bend to push for the summit. I don't have a photo of that day because I too was carrying as little as possible, and hadn't yet finished school. Three long hours of a terrible climb and four hours waiting for three seconds of Anquetil: I thought that was a fair exchange. My bike, lying in the ditch, was still green. Anquetil passed by so quickly I was worried whether or not he had found time to admire the landscape. Everything was so beautiful, so vast, so different. Did he really manage to enjoy it? Did the riders enjoy the beauty of the world around them? Head down on his machine, could he only see a strip of blue sky? Was he condemned to follow Bahamontes' back wheel? Poulidor's buttocks? Did he really like the same bike as me? Was I the stuff from which champion cyclists are made? If he had been standing immobile like me at the roadside, waiting for himself, would he also have felt such tremendous pain in his legs? If for a single moment in my childhood I doubted that I was Anquetil, it was certainly not during the climb to Brunissard, but rather at this fleeting moment of a raging battle, when glory took the shape of a lightning flash.

Les Elfes and the
Shattered Model

And then Anquetil left my childhood universe when I tiptoed out of childhood itself. We had grown older. He had ended his life as a cyclist and I had put an end to my Anquetil life without any violence. Even if I was a little less tubby, I still wasn't blond, still not slender, and on my bike I was still as banal as ever. I didn't even have the grace of someone like Pollentier or Agostinho, who are magnificently ugly on a machine. I was simply banal. Other champions had arrived, whom I admired as an adult, other men and women had emerged from the pages of books and taken me over. Painlessly, I had realised not only that I would never be Anquetil, but that I would not even be a racing cyclist.

I wasn't indifferent to his life, though. I recognised his voice when he commented on races on the TV or radio, and his face when he appeared in the pages of *Paris Match* or *Jours de France*, which my mother had for the customers in her hairdressing saloon. One day I learned that he had had a daughter, and secretly told myself she could have been my friend, possibly my girlfriend. That

I could have emerged from Rouen cathedral on her arm, and become Jacques Anquetil's son-in-law ...

Les Elfes

On 27 December 1969, after an omnium race in the Anvers velodrome, Anquetil and Janine return to Les Elfes. Janine parks the car in front of the shed where Jacques keeps his equipment and, unusually for him, he says he wants to take the two bikes off the roof rack himself. He pushes them alone inside the shed. All his gear is there: frames, wheels, accessories, dozens of tubulars drying on rims, ready to be installed. It's full of souvenirs of races, victories, defeats. A champion's entire life. Jacques carefully hangs the two bikes from their hooks, ready for use. But he will never touch them again.

ANQUETIL: The page has been turned. I have no regrets, just a few pangs now and then, mere details. If I had to rewrite it, I would probably do it all exactly the same way, possibly with a few less steep hills, possibly with me in the lead just once over a col in the Alps or Pyrenees, possibly Paris–Roubaix because I almost won it. But yes, I do have a regret, just one. The rainbow jersey. I love that jersey. I couldn't give a damn about being the world champion, but I would have loved to wear that jersey. It's beautiful, white with coloured stripes. And how happy I would have been to put a clean one on every morning for a year. In the peloton, I always saw it on other riders' backs: Baldini, Darrigade, Janssen, Van Looy, Altig, and repeated the colours to myself: blue, red, black, yellow, green. I dreamt of it, and still do.

⁓

The bike years are over. The car is in the garage, the crazy races across France and Europe are a thing of the past. Janine is no longer the driver. Jacques has turned the heavy page of his cycling career.

Now that he's a pedestrian, in a suit and tie, who is he? Often, it's when they come out of the saddle that the champions' dramas become evident: Ocaña and Koblet who go off the rails and lose their lives. Pantani and Vandenbrouck who seek oblivion in drink and drugs and die from them … Anquetil doesn't change; he doesn't put on weight, he doesn't abandon his aloof elegance or his taste for irony. He accepts the honours and enjoys the comfort he has striven so hard to achieve. He is 35, his legs don't ache any more, and he's already achieved most of his dreams. The adolescent in a hat, his nose stuck in a rose bush as he peered at the bourgeois houses on the banks of the Seine, has become the owner of Les Elfes. 'My dream,' he had admitted a few years earlier, 'is to buy a farm in Normandy and to live there quietly.' Quite a farm: he owns a chateau surrounded by 700 hectares of prime agricultural land …

Situated at La Neuville-Chant-d'Oisel, the mansion is full of history. It once belonged to the Maupassant family, and was where the elite of the arts and sciences of

Rouen used to meet. Gustave Flaubert stayed there regularly. In 1869, the house was bought by Louis Pottevin, a painter and cousin of the writer Guy de Maupassant. It was restored as a chateau in 1874, and was to become the place where the elite of the cycling world was to meet.

Anquetil takes no time off, but immediately settles into the role of gentleman farmer and businessman. He has already been involved for a long while in business, agriculture, stockbreeding, but also real estate, a gravel quarry ... doubtless his declared lack of interest in cycling helps him over this delicate transition. The life of a racing cyclist may be very hard, but it's also very structured, with every minute planned and with little room for improvisation. Anquetil knows he mustn't remain idle, so that he won't be invaded by dark thoughts, uncertain outcomes, unfocused wishes. He gets on with it.

At Les Elfes, he is lord of the manor. Janine and he receive people and, above all, like people to drop in on them. The twelve guest rooms are often full. They have their regulars and others who visit occasionally. Childhood friends like Dieulois and Billaux, 'scribblers' like Chany or Blondin, and, of course, cyclists. The Anquetils are regal, their dinner table is always magnificent, the nights endless. Nostalgia for cycling leads to party after party. These can last for days, but Anquetil always keeps a distance. He likes to see his friends enjoying themselves. He joins in all the games, the fun and all the drinking sessions, he's not the last to evoke memories of the peloton, but he always keeps that slight reserve, that little sliver of solitude that defines him so well.

One day, as a joke and to cock a snook at the great History of Cycling, he organises a lunch for former racers where everyone has to wear the jersey they never won: Poulidor is finally in yellow, Anquetil dons the rainbow jersey of world champion, Altig the pink one from the Giro, etc. Memories from their cycling days are there, ready to pour forth, but they are there also to be made fun of, to play with, to be placed irreverently at their proper level in the destiny of mankind.

⁓

Curiously, together with his work at Les Elfes, Anquetil chooses to remain in cycling. The non-conformist, the renovator, the innovator, the aloof champion, the one who did drugs, succeeds in becoming a member of the Federation and gets to be a selector for the French team. There he proves to be both competent and fairly conservative in his choices. He also stays close to racing as a commentator on Europe No. 1, alongside Fernand Choisel, and then on Antenne 2, alongside Robert Chapatte, as well as for *L'Équipe*, with Philippe Brunel. He doesn't insist on the idea of the 'good old days'. He's completely at home in modern-day cycling – after all, he invented it. His commentaries are sober, delivered in a level, elegant, serious but slightly detached manner that is in sharp contrast to the forced enthusiasm of the usual journalistic commentary. His view of racing seems even clearer than when he himself was riding, but where he is at his most subtle is definitely when he analyses the psychology of champions. He is good about men, and recognises his equals at the first turn of the pedal.

Chapatte particularly remembers the day when Merckx beat the hour record in Mexico and when, thanks to a series of coincidences that left all the other journalists green with envy, Anquetil and he found themselves on their own with the Belgian racer after his achievement, in the comfortable booth reserved for him in the velodrome. Merckx couldn't sit down, and the only words he could say were: 'It hurts'. When asked where, he pointed to his thighs, his back, his neck, his head. Completely forgetting his role as a journalist, Anquetil spoke of his admiration for him but then shouted at him for not being prepared for all the pain. 'I went to Besançon to train, but you just do as you please, you don't make any effort. What a record, what a marvel! You're a blockhead! How stupid you look!' No one else in the world but Anquetil could have got away with telling the great Merckx that he hadn't prepared enough when he had just gone almost 50 kilometres in an hour and was suffering so badly that he kept repeating 'It hurts, it hurts', over and over.

For his part, Fernand Choisel was never astonished at what Anquetil might say alongside him. He knew him too well, and their reactions were too well coordinated for him to be taken by surprise. He does, though, remember that Anquetil was always a man of his word. When he made his second attempt on the world hour record, the start was scheduled for 17.45, which inescapably meant it would end at 18.45. Choisel had agreed with Anquetil that he would open the news programme on Europe No. 1 live at 19.00. After some small hitches, Anquetil had only been able to get started at 17.55. That didn't matter: the feat accomplished, he rushed to the microphone to keep his promise before any of the ceremonies. Choisel wasn't left speechless, but he remembered it well.

⁓

As for me, a modest but attentive TV viewer, if I had to retain only one of Anquetil's commentaries, it would be the one he did at the end of a terrible stage on the cobbles of the North, in 1979. Hinault and Zoetemelk were battling it out. Hinault had lost three minutes 45 seconds and looked completely beaten. Everybody agreed. Anquetil, though, calmly declared: 'There's a kid who's winning the Tour right now, and that's Hinault, because he fought like a dog over 150 kilometres not to lose any more time. He's going to win.' No one but Anquetil could have seen that.

In October 1969, at the moment when Anquetil is about to retire, the magazine *Miroir du cyclisme* publishes a special large-format issue entitled 'Jacques Anquetil's prodigious career' with a cover portrait of my hero on a black background. I buy it at the first kiosk I come across and devour the articles, interviews, testimonies from other riders, trainers, friends and foes. I also dwell on the photographs, race photos most of which I was already familiar with: Paris–Roubaix and his face covered in mud, a lap of honour brandishing a bouquet of flowers he doesn't know what to do with, a wonderful profile shot in the Vigorelli velodrome of him in front of the clock with the yellow jersey and the number one pinned to his chest, and photos outside cycling that I know less well: Anquetil in a plain suit or with pin-stripes, a flowery tie and a white shirt with a pointed collar, dressed up to the nines, signet ring on his finger and always, as a souvenir, his chronometer on his right wrist. And then, on page 51, opposite an interview about his profession with Maurice Vidal from 1964, a larger than life-size portrait that I don't know. This photo opens a door inside me. It tells me secrets the others don't reveal. It shows the whole mystery of Anquetil. It's an image following great effort, a day of sunshine and sweat, a day of anguish, perplexity, of reflection and fear. A troubling photo. One eye is in darkness, the other is fixed on some mysterious problem. Anquetil doesn't know he is being photographed, otherwise he would never have let so much of himself come through, so much fragility and doubt. This is the secret man one can only guess at, the one the magazine doesn't even mention, the one Anquetil himself isn't sure he wants to know. It's this photo that makes me want to get my own unguarded photo of him one day.

Affairs of the heart are complicated at Les Elfes. For a long while, there were only rumours and hints from people who claimed to know what was going on but didn't really want to tell in case the facts proved them wrong, and also by people who really knew and wanted to keep quiet about it. This *omerta* was especially true of the inner circle. Until much later on, when Sophie Anquetil, Jacques' daughter, decided to reveal everything in a lively, loving book entitled *Pour l'amour de Jacques* (*For the Love of Jacques*), in which she conceals nothing of what she knows. Since she was the baby of the story, it's plain that she doesn't know everything, and her tale has, despite her, something of the 'official version' about it. But it also has an air of complete freedom and openness, which leads you to think she has often hit the mark.

In fact, it's a simple story. After ending his cycling career, Anquetil wants to have a child. He has brought up his wife's two children, but he wants one of his own. Janine can no longer have children. After first thinking of using a surrogate mother, it is decided he will have one with Annie, Janine's daughter. She agrees. There are still shady areas surrounding this decision that to outside eyes can seem risky. Is Janine the driver yet again, pushing Jacques into the arms of her daughter? Or is it love that is in the driving seat? Was love really a surprise guest, or had it been lurking in the chateau for quite a while? This could well be the case. Annie has always adored Jacques, and has grown into a beautiful, attractive young woman. Anquetil appreciates women – and is appreciated by them in return. Why would he not react to his stepdaughter? When I ask Sophie Anquetil this on the telephone, she tells me she has just found some Super 8 family films shot at Les Elfes. In one of them you can see her mother, who must be twelve or thirteen years' old at the time, fluttering round Jacques: 'She wouldn't leave him alone, she was all over him, she already wanted him.'

The question remains unresolved, but Sophie did have two mothers. Jacques makes a strange decision: if having a child with Annie seems like a natural, comprehensible choice, wanting to pretend Janine is the mother is far less clear. 'My father decided when I was born that to everyone else I would be the daughter not of Annie my real mother but of Nanou, my grandmother', writes Sophie. 'I was a little girl with two mothers. One of my mothers was the daughter of the other one, and my two mothers were at the same time, and for almost fifteen years, under the same roof together; the two wives of my bigamist papa.' One can imagine just what a time bomb this must have been. Seen from the outside, even if it's not a question of incest, it's terribly confused. Seen from the inside, the rivalry must logically soon become unbearable. And yet Anquetil and doubtless the baby Sophie keep it up for fifteen years! Sophie writes that Jacques would start the night with Annie and end it with Janine, while she made the opposite journey from one bed to the other. Here too, Anquetil proves how unique he is, and the strange power he had over others.

I'm leafing through a colour magazine, *Paris Match*, which presents Jacques Anquetil in his chateau. In it you can see Les Elfes, the beautiful lawns, the big swimming pool, the deck chairs; everyone is smiling and posing, dressed in summer shirts and dresses. It seems like one long holiday. I read the captions, but they are of no interest to a bike lover, then force myself to read the article itself. Naturally enough, it's tepid stuff: 'everyone is so nice, so charming', but then at the end of a paragraph I learn that the chateau Les Elfes once belonged to the Maupassant family. That brings me up sharp. I could almost say it stops me in my tracks. It has to be said that by now I have grown. I have read *Bel-Ami* and *Boule de Suif* and several other books by Guy de Maupassant. All of a sudden, it's as if I'd been given the key to the cellars. I've just stumbled on the secret passage between my decision to become a writer and my dream of being a racing cyclist. It's this improbable link between Maupassant and Anquetil, the two giants fighting it out inside me.

⁓

It's a calm autumn night, but inside the chateau, the women are going at it hammer and tongs. Anquetil knows there'll be no more peace. He knows competition too well not to understand that the first who wants to remain first and the second who wants to become first will only become allies in order to neutralise the third. He knows it means heartbreak for him, and that there will never again be peace in Les Elfes. If his heart doesn't fail him altogether, he'll have to tear it out, and afterwards he'll always be bleeding.

He picks up little Sophie, who has already heard too much. The night outside is cold, so he protects her under his jacket. They plunge into the dark forest, on the trail of silence and the night creatures. His head flashlight shows them the way, the torch in his hand reveals nooks and crannies. He searches in the undergrowth, studies the tracks on the wet path. He regains his calm, and slows down. He takes Sophie by the hand and helps her look more closely.

'Look,' he says, coming to a halt. 'The prints of a hare. Is it male or female?'

Sophie has learned her lesson well. She can see that the prints left by the back legs are faint, scarcely stronger than those left by the front legs …

'It's a lady', she says proudly.

Jacques shines a light on her face and kisses her on the forehead.

'Now let's go and see the big beasts of the undergrowth. Crouch down, pass underneath, I'll hold the brambles away from you.'

'We ought to come and clear it with Bubull.'

'Would you like someone to come and destroy your house with a bulldozer? These bushes belong to the wild boar; it's where they live and we have to leave them in peace. Look.'

Anquetil stamps his foot and rustles the leaves. Not exactly scared, the boars trot across the beam of light. Sophie presses herself against him.

On another night, Anquetil looks for peace in the dark sky. He's on the roof with his daughter. They are wearing their anoraks. He unfolds the charts, adjusts the telescope and starts telling her the stories of the stars. Then they count them together, and look for the constellations. Anquetil knows them by heart. The vault of heaven has become the realm through which he'll never ride. After spending his first life with his head down, he now ruins his sight with telescopes and has his head in the stars, aiming at an imaginary and doubtless magical world that has become familiar to him. Beside him, Sophie raises her eyes. The night sky isn't her world, but she's a little girl who is happy to be looking in the same direction as her papa.

One day, unable to be 'the only one', Annie leaves and shatters the balance in the chateau. She leaves not only Sophie, but also a wound so deep in Jacques' heart that the old order can never be re-established. Janine will have to leave as well, bringing to a close a lavish story of love and sharing. Later on, Jacques will find a new balance when he marries Dominique, who was part of the family, and has a son, Christopher, with her. He won't live to see his son grow up, because he soon falls victim to cancer. 'Yes, I have stomach cancer. I'm going on the slab in Rouen after the Tour de France. But don't pull a face like that, you can live a long time without a stomach.' Not always ...

The shattered model

As a sport, cycling is lucky. It has a long-lasting, privi-leged relationship with the media. The written press suits it perfectly, radio is ideal for it, and television fits it like a glove. It has to be said that cycling, especially when it comes to the important Tours, combines the elegance of a feuilleton and the seduction of a tourist brochure. In this context, its champions get their share of glory. And among them, Anquetil has been particularly spoilt. He was the last great champion of the written tradition: for the greater part of his career, he could count on the ser-vices of two of the finest pens in the history of cycling journalism, Pierre Chany and Antoine Blondin. The first of these is a model of precision. He has no equal in giving races a start, middle and end, to extract the essence of each and every event, and to situate every single hill in the overall history of cycling. Blondin is the bottle imp, the perfect writer. His prose sparkles, and he sprinkles the peloton with his wit to make it shine. They are on Anquetil's side, and count themselves as his friends. They help him emerge from many a difficult situation smelling of roses. More than that, when necessary they know how to put a flea in his ear and give him a good kick up the backside, pretending they are angry with him. But they have well and truly understood that they need one another, and that everything always ends up as polished articles in *L'Equipe* (those were the days when there was more to read in that newspaper). Their shared story is that of a long friendship; for anyone wishing to follow the Great Jacques' career step by step, Chany's articles still offer the most valuable insights. Blondin's quips often shed light on Anquetil as a man. Wasn't he the one who summed up the Anquetil-Poulidor rivalry by declaring that Anquetil was Gothic and Poulidor Romanesque?

When asked how the day's racing had been for him, Anquetil, who as we know showed little interest in the details of a race, was in the habit of saying: 'Go ask Chany. I was just pedalling. I'm more accustomed to racing my life than to writing it.'

It's true that in general cyclists don't know how to describe their races. One could swear they hadn't been there. Blinded behind a wall of bent backs, blinkered by a horizon of buttocks. Now they're in the lead, now they're at the back … After the finish line, they exit the stage as quickly as they can. The next day, they recount what they did exactly as they've read in the newspaper. Part of this lack of spontaneous lucidity comes from the way their minds are clouded by the pills and injections that blur their sense of the race. Amphetamines are the enemy of memory. They efface not only the bad moments but the good ones too. A shame. Which gives rise to the crazy desire to do better next time – which in fact means 'to remember the next time, and to tell it better'.

It's very easy then to know everything about Anquetil. But the more you learn, the more the mystery deepens. Anquetil cannot be a model.

To want to be Proust when you set out on your literary career is understandable but catastrophic. (Worse still would be Queneau.) To want to be Anquetil if one is

131

a cyclist is an even more dreadful idea. Wanting to be the opposite of Anquetil would be just as counter-productive. However much you may want to be like the older person you admire, however attracted you are to him and the perfect model he represents for you, it's wiser to see him as an adversary.

That's what Anquetil did so magnificently with Coppi when he went to see him in his early days as a champion. If he had so wished, he could have learnt all the *campionissimo's* secrets, snuggle under his wing, learn the lesson, let the giant Cavanna feel his way to sculpting his body, mould him into the shape of the master. Instead, Anquetil chose to go and see Coppi to tell him in the friendliest way possible that he was going to be his opponent and intended to eclipse him.

The greatest champions have a taste for solitude. They are often far ahead, drawn on by the summits and indifferent to the pack who, far behind them, try to help each other keep up and to overcome gravity. In their solitary effort, these champions are alone with themselves. Sometimes too, they are alone, behind the rest, fast asleep. Most of the time, even in the midst of the peloton, they are alone. Of all these solitary champions, Anquetil was without doubt the most solitary of all, the strongest, the most exposed. Between the ages of six and nineteen, I was Anquetil and I can testify that it wasn't a comfortable place to be; it was simply mission impossible.

I remember that I cried the day Anquetil decided to abandon the Tour de France – to abandon the Tour and cycling. I imagined he would do it head held high, perched on the top of the world, like Bobet who had taken his bow at the summit of Mont Iseran. No such thing: Anquetil finished in an obscure rain puddle. He stopped there, paralysed with fear, in the middle of a descent, with a cold storm raging. I shared that freezing cold for a moment. Something inside me froze: perhaps it was simply my youth, or the absurd desire to be someone else.

Many years later, the question Geminiani posed remains unanswered: 'If he had been like the others, would he have been better or worse?' The question remains unanswered because it is stupid. Anquetil raced like nobody else, and lived the same way. An impossible model to follow in both cases.

One thing remains certain: he didn't manage to escape the curse of the Tour's yellow jerseys. They may earn the right to eternity through their exploits, but definitely not their longevity. Like many of them, Anquetil dies young. He is 53. He is younger than Bobet, who dies aged 58, but older than Fignon, dead at 50, or Coppi, at 41, or Koblet, at 39 …

❧

The first time I saw Anquetil for real, I must have been only ten or so, because there was still a velodrome on Rue Papin in Saint-Étienne, where I was growing up on my little bike. In my memory, I can still hear the wood of that velodrome creaking under the weight of spectators, and I can still see the mattress of smoke stuck to the ceiling, since back then nobody yet lived without a Gauloise or maize-paper Gitane stuck to their bottom lip. I didn't smoke. My father had got us tickets trackside, in a box at the top of a bend. We shared it with a strange little woman from the town, dressed in black, looking out of place and modest in this noisy world of male supporters. A few minutes later, when he came on his bike to give her a hug, she turned out to be none other than the mother of Roger Rivière, the Lord of the Ring. During the warm-up, he came and stopped right in front of us, seizing the guardrail and leaning over to her. She laid an affectionate hand on his thigh. He called her 'maman'. 'It doesn't matter if you don't win,' she said in her fine Saint-Étienne accent, 'but make sure you don't fall.'

The track stretched down from me like a ravine, a slope definitely not for cyclists. My father explained it was made of maple, planed and patiently smoothed by contact with the helium-filled silk tubulars. He assured me that Robert Chapatte, a track expert, had said it was very quick: 'one of the quickest in Europe'. I couldn't imagine how an unmoving track could be quick: to me it was only the racers who had the privilege of speed.

The contest was between the French and the Italians, with Anquetil and Rivière on one side, Coppi and Faggin on the other. They had to compete in three categories: an in-line race, a time trial and a pursuit. I only had eyes for Anquetil, his chest parallel with his green bike frame, majestically immobile, pale and blond.

The public, though, was all for Roger Rivière, the child prodigy from the black country, the young ace who was going to sweep everyone before him. An exceptional racer, rapid up mountains, irresistible on the track, resilient, he was destined for every colour of jersey – pink, yellow and rainbow, in the cycling world.

In the in-line race, when Rivière was up against Fausto Coppi, he forced him into a game of crawling along, one of those painful episodes that stretch muscles and nerves until one of the two cyclists gives in and decides to take the other one on his wheel, towards almost certain victory. To accomplish this masterpiece of muscular patience, Rivière had again come to place himself in front of his mother, in front of me. She briefly touched his jersey. I didn't.

Anquetil was keeping himself back for the pursuit. When his turn came, he was marvellous. In my memory, his image is startlingly clear: he is a pale, shining blur; his decisive acceleration still makes my thighs ache, just as he did those of the great Fausto Coppi. He pursued him and almost caught him up before the race was over. He also won two straight in-line races against Faggin, which allowed France to triumph over Italy.

This meet has remained so deeply engraved on my young boy's memory that I have talked to my father about it a thousand times, recounted it a hundred times to my friends. Thirty years later I even made a short story of it, in my collection *Les athlètes dans leur tête*.

⌒

As I write these words now, more than 50 years after

the events, I feel the need to develop things a little, to glean another anecdote from the race. So I visit the Saint-Étienne town archives to consult newspapers from the period. It's snowing. The receptionist says I'm very brave. I'm all alone in the big, silent reading room. I am brought the copies of *Le Tribune* and *Le Progrès* that I've asked for.

The heavy binding cracks, the smell of paper wafts up from the pages. They have turned yellow, are a bit brittle, the photographs are blurred. Maybe I'll find an image of myself, tiny alongside Mme Rivière, perhaps a victory shot of Anquetil. I search the pages of the day in question, then the ones from the day before, the following day. The competition is described in great detail, but the two newspapers are categorical: Anquetil wasn't there.

❧

There was indeed an omnium race between France and Italy on 12 October 1958. But on the French side, backing up Roger Rivière, the cyclists were Darrigade and Gaignard ... I can't believe my eyes: more research convinces me that, on the day of that meet, Jacques Anquetil could not possibly have been present, because he was beating the immense Gérard Saint in the Grand Prix of Lugano!

So it was a phantom I saw race, pedalling for all he was worth, as beautiful as a Caravel, and I admired him. I had an athlete inside my head. The image of Anquetil on the maple-wood track at the Vel d'Hiv in Saint-Étienne has stayed with me for more than 50 years. It was the basis of my 'Anquetil passion', and yet it was nothing more than an image. In his barrel chest, in his terrifying leg and back muscles, Anquetil was hiding some of the stuff of which my dreams are woven. Perhaps, in the end, his greatest secret was to appear everywhere he was not.